COACHING SWIMMING
SUCCESSFULLY
SECOND EDITION

Dick Hannula

Human Kinetics

Library of Congress Cataloging-in-Publication Data

Hannula, Dick, 1928-
  Coaching swimming successfully / Dick Hannula.— 2nd ed.
    p. cm.
Includes index.
  ISBN 0-7360-4519-8 (Soft cover)
  1. Swimming—Coaching. I. Title.
  GV837.65 .H35 2003
  797.2'1—dc21
                                                              2002153243

ISBN: 0-7360-4519-8

Acquisitions Editor: Martin Barnard
Production Editor: Melinda Graham
Assistant Editor: John Wentworth
Copyeditor: Julie Anderson
Proofreader: Kathy Bennett
Indexer: Betty Frizzell
Graphic Designer: Nancy Rasmus
Photo Manager: Dan Wendt
Cover Designer: Jack W. Davis
Photographer (cover): Getty Images
Photographers (interior): pages 38, 41, 47, 83, and 107 ©Empics; all others by James M. Fredrickson and James C. Fredrickson
Illustrator: Jim Boettcher
Printer: Versa Press

Human Kinetics books are available at special discounts for bulk purchase. Special editions or book excerpts can also be created to specification. For details, contact the Special Sales Manager at Human Kinetics.

Printed in the United States of America   10 9 8 7 6 5 4 3 2 1

Human Kinetics
Web site: www.HumanKinetics.com

United States: Human Kinetics
P.O. Box 5076
Champaign, IL 61825-5076
800-747-4457
e-mail: humank@hkusa.com

Canada: Human Kinetics
475 Devonshire Road Unit 100
Windsor, ON N8Y 2L5
800-465-7301 (in Canada only)
e-mail: orders@hkcanada.com

Europe: Human Kinetics
107 Bradford Road
Stanningley
Leeds LS28 6AT, United Kingdom
+44 (0) 113 255 5665
e-mail: hk@hkeurope.com

Australia: Human Kinetics
57A Price Avenue
Lower Mitcham, South Australia 5062
08 8277 1555
e-mail: liahka@senet.com.au

New Zealand: Human Kinetics
P.O. Box 105-231, Auckland Central
09-523-3462
e-mail: hkp@ihug.co.nz

Dedicated to my wife and partner, Sylvia, our children, and grandchildren

CONTENTS

Foreword by Teri McKeever vii

Acknowledgments ix

Introduction xi

Part I   Coaching Foundation   1

Chapter 1   Developing a Swimming Coaching Philosophy .. 3
Chapter 2   Communicating Your Approach 9
Chapter 3   Motivating Swimmers 19
Chapter 4   Building a Swimming Program 31

Part II   Coaching Stroke Technique   41

Chapter 5   Basic Principles in Teaching Strokes 43
Chapter 6   Dolphin or Butterfly Kick 51
Chapter 7   Crawl Stroke 57
Chapter 8   Backstroke 75
Chapter 9   Breaststroke 87
Chapter 10   Butterfly 101

Part III   Coaching Plans   111

Chapter 11   Planning Training 113
Chapter 12   Preparing for Practices 127

Part IV   Coaching Meets   139

Chapter 13   Preparing for Meets 141

Chapter 14   Handling Meets 151

Part V Coaching Evaluation   159

Chapter 15   Evaluating Swimmers' Performance 161

Chapter 16   Evaluating Your Program 167

Index 173

About the Author 179

FOREWORD

In the second edition of *Coaching Swimming Successfully*, Coach Dick Hannula continues to expand and develop the coaching principles that have led him in his unparalleled coaching career. His accomplishments on the deck are well documented and stand above those of his peers. In "retirement" he has continued to positively impact the swimming community.

I appreciate Coach Hannula's attention to the aspects of coaching beyond the X's and O's. These intangibles will distinguish the good coach from the great coach and the good teams from the exceptional ones. As coaches, we have a unique opportunity and responsibility to positively impact our athletes well beyond their swimming abilities. This will be among our greatest successes and Coach Hannula's career documents this very fact. His success and legacy are no accident—they are a result of years of thoughtful preparation and purposeful action. He has shared many of his insights in the hope that you too will benefit from his life experiences.

Coaching Swimming Successfully presents both fundamental and advanced principles in a format that is appropriate for all levels of coaches, from the beginning coach to the most seasoned veteran. Additionally, this edition has expanded technical information with terrific illustrations that make it a useful teaching tool. This book is not just for coaches; swimmers alike will benefit from its content.

I encourage you to read this valuable book and use it as a resource for your own journey to success!

Teri McKeever
Head Coach, Women's Swimming and Diving
University of California at Berkeley

ACKNOWLEDGMENTS

Thanks to the coaches who reviewed my work and provided many positive suggestions that I incorporated into the second edition of *Coaching Swimming Successfully*. Ron Johnson (retired, Arizona State University), George Block (Alamo Area Aquatics), Bob Miller (Bellevue Club and Tucson Jewish Community Center), Rick Klatt (Fresno Dolphins Swim Team), and Jay Benner (Tacoma Swim Club) were very helpful to me in writing a better book.

I also want to thank the artist illustrator, Jim Boettcher. He was an assistant coach with me and an art teacher at Wilson High School. I am also very appreciative of James M. Fredrickson and James C. Fredrickson, the father and son photographer team. James M. was our team photographer at Wilson High School and Tacoma Swim Club for about 20 years, and James C. was a very good swimmer for both of my teams.

INTRODUCTION

My first teaching and swim coaching job was at Lincoln High School in Tacoma, Washington. I was fresh out of college with about six years of limited high school and college swimming experience. I was the head coach and the only coach, and I learned mostly by trial and error those first couple of years. At that time, very little coaching material was available: one or two books that contained only minimum information. Swimming publications were nonexistent. Any social event of coaches at a swimming competition became a "clinic." We learned by doing and by asking questions of other successful coaches.

Now we have excellent organized regional and national coaching clinics. Several professional coaching and governing organizations offer educational, safety, and certification courses. Coaching publications, videos, and books are available. In short, new coaches can come up to speed in a much shorter period of time than when I became a coach.

I've spent more than 50 years in coaching. When you add six years of competitive swimming prior to becoming a coach, it becomes obvious that I've had considerable experience. You can safely assume that I'm not a kid in years. However, I feel like a kid through my association with young swimmers. A few years ago, I retired from club coaching at Tacoma Swim Club. I didn't really get away from this great sport of swimming. Within six months, I became a volunteer coach with our club senior team. I assist Jay Benner, our new head coach, as he needs me and depending on my availability. One of the main areas has been in the teaching of correct stroke technique. This is the best of both worlds: I still love the sport and helping swimmers become the best that they can be, yet I have the freedom of other retirement pursuits.

One of the benefits of my retirement has been to attend several international coaching clinics and to visit the training sites and observe some of the world's best swimmers in training. Meeting and talking to successful coaches within the United States and on the international level has also helped prepare me to write this book.

It has been almost 10 years since the first edition of *Coaching Swimming Successfully*. This revision reflects many stroke training and technique guidelines. In most respects, this is a new book. It is designed to help every coach provide an exciting, positive, and rewarding experience for his or her swimmers. I've tried to cover all aspects of coaching by reliving my own coaching experiences. In addition,

I believe that every swimmer would accelerate his or her own development and commitment to swimming by reading this book.

As swimming coaches, we have the unique opportunity to develop strong, motivated leaders who will continue to lead in other areas outside the sport. Winning, in the pool and life, is being the best that you can be. Measure what can be measured, and measure against yourself. Swimmers learn great health habits. They have the opportunity to be the fittest of the fit.

After more than 50 years of coaching swimming, I'm still thrilled to be part of the swimmer development process. The committed swimmer loves the challenge of training and competition. Coaching is the key that turns this process into reality. Be a coach and not a critic, and you will be in the sport for the long haul. I hope that *Coaching Swimming Successfully* can be your model.

Part I

COACHING FOUNDATION

Chapter
1

DEVELOPING A SWIMMING COACHING PHILOSOPHY

Your philosophy is the set of principles or ethics that you live by. Vince Lombardi was quoted as saying that the only concerns in his life and the lives of his players should be God, family, and the Green Bay Packers, in that order. My teams may not be the Packers, but they are that important to me, as your teams should be to you. I must care about all of the swimmers on my team, whether they are the fastest or the slowest. The faces may change each year, but my philosophy remains the same.

A swimming coach's success is measured by the progress and the development of his or her swimmers. Although you may have a limited talent pool to draw from, the athletes who make up your team should reflect the teaching, training, and discipline that you've given them. This reflection is made visible by their actions in and out of the pool.

Your philosophy must be centered in belief. If you believe totally in your basic philosophy, then it has the roots necessary to ensure a lasting commitment. Continuity in your core beliefs, your philosophy, is necessary to gain the respect of your team members and their parents. You must be totally committed to your beliefs; otherwise, your philosophy won't stand up through adversity or failure.

In this chapter I present the principles that form the foundation of my philosophy, and I describe how I share that philosophy through the goals I establish for my swimming program. Remember that my philosophy influences all phases of my coaching, just as your outlook affects your actions.

Every coach must determine his or her own philosophy—the unwavering principles that will provide consistency and clarity in decision making. All of the most successful coaches in our sport, from Peter Daland, George Haines, and Doc

Counsilman to Mark Schubert, Eddie Reese, Skip Kenney, and Richard Quick, have demonstrated the importance of leading a swimming program with a steady and clear vision.

Origin of a Philosophy

Your philosophy of coaching is developed from your own experiences, both in swimming and in life. Experiences specific to your swimming coaching philosophy would include these:

- Books and magazine articles you have read
- Videos you have watched
- Clinics you have attended
- Experiences you have had as a swimmer and a swim coach
- Conversations you have had with athletes and coaching colleagues
- Observations you have made of other coaches at training or competitions

Many coaches have had the invaluable opportunity to intern with an experienced and successful coach. I have had many young coaches intern with me, for periods ranging from two weeks to nine months. Other coaches have told me about spending a week or more just watching the training sessions of a successful coach. Even veteran coaches like me can learn by watching successful coaches train swimmers their way in their own pool.

Learning Opportunities

You will never have enough experience from just your own program. You need to get "outside the box" occasionally. One of my best learning opportunities was to visit several successful coaches and observe their training sessions over a few days. I observed Richard Quick and Skip Kenney at Stanford University. I also went to a training session at the University of California, Berkeley, with Nort Thornton. I came back from that trip with many new and useful ideas that improved my program.

Another major opportunity to watch successful coaches is at the national championships. At the first national championship meets I attended, I had the opportunity to watch great coaches and swimmers in action. At my first national championship, I watched the coach and his world record holder work on the backstroke in the warm-up pool. They used drills to improve technique at the championship meet. I catalogued those drills for extensive use with my swimmers in our training sessions. These drills were new to me and proved very successful for my backstroke swimmers the next season.

Such learning opportunities are all around you, so take advantage of them when they present themselves. I have never found a successful swim coach who wasn't willing to share ideas.

All of your experiences with other coaches will factor into the development of your philosophical base. I encourage you to keep adding to that base through your contacts with the many excellent former and active swim coaches available to you.

A swimming coach's success is measured by the progress and the development of his or her swimmers.

Defining Your Philosophy

Every coach must develop a philosophy that will be the base for coaching decisions. My philosophy grew from three key sources. One was Coach Howard Firby of Canada, who was the greatest teacher of stroke fundamentals that I've known. He impressed on me the need to teach technique effectively to achieve any success as a swim coach.

Another source was Coach John Tallman, formerly of the University of Washington. John was a scientist long before science entered into swim coaching. Always challenging and forming new ideas, John made me aware and appreciative of changes in coaching.

The third source was my friend Bob Miller, who coached in Seattle and Bellevue, Washington. Bob, himself an athlete, had the ability to train hard and to challenge his swimmers accordingly. Through him I learned to better appreciate the value of hard work in swimming success.

After more than 40 years of coaching swimming, I have developed six equally important tenets for my philosophy. (You may add or subtract from these in defining your own philosophy.)

1. **There is no substitute for hard work.** All swimmers must invest time and effort in the sport. Success in competition is the direct result of how much work each individual puts into it. Similarly, there are no shortcuts for a coach. Consistent and persistent effort by athletes and coaches is a prerequisite for achieving anything worthwhile in swimming.

2. **Every athlete counts.** A team is only as strong as its weakest link. You must be concerned about the attitude and the improvement of every team member. Team strength comes from raising the standards of all team members.

3. **Winning is not just being Number 1.** Every swimmer on your team can be and should be a winner. A winner sets goals and then strives to attain them. Both swimmers and coaches who continue to strive for their goals are winners. Winning must be measured against one meaningful and reliable standard—yourself. As the coach, you have to accept this philosophy of winning and educate your swimmers and their parents accordingly.

4. **Responsibility is required.** The greatest power you have is the ability to choose. However, your choices require responsibility. Because you choose to coach, you are responsible for your team's results. Similarly, because your swimmers choose to be on the team, they must accept the responsibilities of their choice. Your swimmers can choose to study for an exam or to watch television during their available study time. While in training, your swimmers can choose to get the necessary sleep each night or they can decide to stay up late and report to practice tired. In any case, your swimmers must bear the responsibility for choices they make.

5. **Teach first and train second.** Keep returning to basics. All swimmers must establish good technique before they can train effectively.

6. **Change is necessary.** In coaching, change is a fact of life. The athletes you work with and the "best" ways to teach and to train them will change. Such variations are sometimes necessary for your own motivation.

A Change Isn't Always Forever

One very successful year, our team used a method of cycle training that was the result of a college class called Physiology and the Swimming Coach. The following year we intended to follow the same procedure, but after the first week I called my team together and told them I couldn't get excited about the same program again this year. We all agreed and had a more successful year because of the meaningful changes made in the program.

One key to longevity in coaching is adapting to change. Programs need to be dynamic to maintain the enthusiasm of the athletes and the coach.

BE COMFORTABLE AND BE YOURSELF

Though your philosophy may change somewhat over your years of coaching, the core of your philosophy—those tenets that revolve around your value system and that comprise what you want your swimmers to receive from your program—probably won't change. For your basic philosophy to be comfortable, it will have to conform to your value system.

You need to be yourself, so don't adopt a philosophy that isn't you. Be the best that you can be and do it your way. Each coach will have his or her own style of teaching, communicating, and motivating swimmers. Copying some other coach's style won't necessarily work best for you. You have your own unique style, so develop it and make it the best for you.

Stay Hungry

You will never learn all there is to learn about coaching swimming. Be eager to learn throughout your coaching career, because the coach who thinks that she or he knows it all is on a downhill slide. Learning opportunities are all around you, so learn to recognize them and use them.

Go a Step Beyond

We have the opportunity to be a strong and positive influence on the young people we coach. We can't betray the great amount of trust they place in us. We must never lose sight of the great impact that we have on our athletes' lives. Beyond developing their technical and competitive skills, we, as coaches, have a responsibility to our athletes.

It gives coaches great satisfaction when former swimmers keep in touch throughout their lives. An invitation to a wedding or to a college graduation (in my case it is often for one of my swimmers' children) reminds you of your responsibility to make swimming a very positive experience in your swimmers' lives.

Give Equal Opportunity, Not Equal Time

What I have found to be more important and practical than giving equal time is giving each athlete equal opportunity to take advantage of my desire to work with all of them. Those who are willing to give more of themselves in training and competition gain the most benefit from my coaching efforts.

IMPORTANT BELIEFS

I am not suggesting that you adopt my coaching principles—you must feel comfortable with and committed to your own set of beliefs—but I am recommending that you recognize how critical your beliefs are to your coaching. Every day you will be selling your athletes on the things you believe in, and like most coaches and athletes, you believe in those things that you have seen work. The more you see something succeed, the more confident you become—the stronger your belief—that it will succeed again.

As a coach you must develop a philosophy, teaching method, and training program that you believe in totally. Then you must impress on everyone associated with your program that this belief is well founded. Only then will you gain the full commitment of your athletes.

However, this is only the groundwork. If your athletes are to achieve the highest level of performance, you must help them believe they can reach the top. Each swimmer attaining even a personal best performance time at the right moment can help make believers out of his or her teammates.

The following poem was given to me and our team as we prepared for the summer championship meets almost 30 years ago. I don't know the author, but the young woman was a college swimmer training with me for that summer. I have made copies for our team members yearly since that time.

BELIEVE in yourself
and in your dream
though impossible things may seem
someday, somehow you'll get through
to the goal you have in view.

Mountains fall and seas divide
before the one who in her stride
takes the hard road day by day,
sweeping obstacles away.

BELIEVE in yourself and in your plan,
say not—I cannot—but, I CAN.
The prizes of life we fail to win
because we doubt the power within.

BELIEVE

Think Titles

After winning more than a decade of consecutive state boys' championships at Wilson High School, we had not placed one boy in the finals of the U.S. National Senior Championship meet. We were qualifying boys but not placing them at the meet. We were successful at our state level but not at the national level.

Finally one of our swimmers qualified for the finals at the U.S. Senior National Championship meet. I will always remember the surprised look on the faces of the other team members at that meet. For the first time I realized that they did not expect to place or to win at the national championship meet. They were satisfied to just be able to attend the meet. We had talked about it, but very few believed it could happen. This was the breakthrough we needed. In that meet two additional boys placed in the finals in their individual events. These swimmers believed and expected the best at their state high school meet and at their regional competition. It took one tough team member to get the others to believe in themselves and to succeed at the national level.

SETTING GOALS

Goals are an extension of your philosophy. They represent the standards that you believe are important and possible. Some goals will be more important to you than others; for example, your philosophy might say that academic achievement takes precedence over athletic achievement. If an athlete's schoolwork is going to be compromised by an athletic event or training, then academic achievement must come first.

In our program we make the connection between philosophy and goals through our mission statement. We tailor this statement each year to meet the specific abilities and personalities of the athletes on the team. The core of the philosophy—what we value most—does not change.

Your success in attaining your goals, not necessarily how much you achieve, will determine how satisfied you are in your coaching position. Percy Cerutty, the great Australian track coach, said, "To be satisfied is to be finished." If you set your sights low and you reach them, you may feel satisfied, but you probably haven't gained much. However, if you set your sights high and come up a little short, you may not be completely satisfied but you may have made a significant accomplishment.

In chapter 3 I explain how to set goals with your team that are ultimately challenging yet also satisfying. I will distinguish between being satisfied and keeping some gratification in the proper perspective. Goal setting is an important process, because it is a means of establishing tangible aspirations that are consistent with your philosophy, principles, and beliefs.

SUMMARY

Coaching and participation in swimming can be very worthwhile if the outlook and expectations of those involved center on what is best for the athletes. In this chapter I presented the means through which coaches can shape their programs to meet the needs of their athletes:

1. Make the athletes on each year's team second only to family.

2. Continue to learn from every means available, such as clinics, videos, articles, books, coaching colleagues, and your athletes.

3. Determine what values are critical to the development of your athletes.

4. Identify the principles you will use to best convey your philosophy.

5. Commit yourself to your principles, and convince your athletes to share your beliefs.

Chapter 2

COMMUNICATING YOUR APPROACH

Knowledge and experience are important ingredients of successful coaching. However, success depends on the coach's ability to communicate effectively with his or her team members. Good thoughts and ideas must be delivered or they are worthless. You may have the most up-to-date, scientific, and technical information available, and you may know the best there is to know in coaching, but if you do not communicate all that information to your athletes, what good is it? Communication is the key.

This is the *X* factor in coaching. The ability to communicate effectively determines in large part the success of any coach; it is a skill that can and must be developed throughout your career.

Your style of communication may change as necessary to get your view across. Motivation, discussed in detail in chapter 3, is directly related to communication. The ability to get your ideas across to your swimmers will help to build motivation in all parts of your program.

Successful coaches have a number of identifiable traits, the most important of which is enthusiasm. My first high school teaching and coaching job was at Lincoln High School in Tacoma, Washington, which was an old school, built about 1911. It had a motto on the wall that read, "Nothing can be accomplished without enthusiasm." Great coaches communicate with enthusiasm. They know where they're going, and they know what needs to be done to get there.

Enthusiasm is contagious. It affects attitude, work ethics, and a swimmer's personal pride.

GOOD ADVICE

In the early '70s, one of my summer college swimmers who had already won an Olympic medal for another club, and who swam for the national champion University of Indiana, taught me the importance of enthusiasm. After his second season with me, just before he graduated from college, he said to me, "Coach, don't ever lose your enthusiasm!" He said that my enthusiasm had the greatest effect on him as a swimmer. Though a lot of years have gone by, his advice may be some of the best I've ever received.

COMMUNICATING WITH SWIMMERS

You have beliefs that are vital to your program's success. What is the most effective training for particular events? What is the most efficient technique for each stroke and for each individual? You continually communicate such beliefs to your swimmers, sometimes on the team level and sometimes on the individual level. Whatever methods you choose to convey your beliefs, you must reach the highest percentage possible of the swimmers on your team.

For example, I have to express to my swimmers the importance and necessity of individualization of training groups. Sometimes each group will have its own special training; some groups may swim less distance or fewer sprints than another. I must make every team member understand that special training is in the best interests of our team to prepare each group for the specific needs of their particular events. Team unity and cooperation are the results of effective communication.

Early season communication could include many of the following:

- The competitive meet schedule
- Attendance policies
- Team standards
- The seasonal training plan
- Warm-up and cool-down procedures
- Goal-setting procedures

Once you've set your schedule, give it to your swimmers and their parents. In one of the first team meetings, discuss and explain the schedule. Address such matters as when the team must be ready to swim fast and how they must prepare to reach that goal.

Communication will be necessary throughout the season to keep the team and its members directed toward that championship meet at the end of the season. It is a challenge for the coach to anticipate every swimmer's needs to avoid problems. Everyone must be reminded occasionally of the why, where, and how of the program's direction.

Real communication is a product of trust. Find a way to convince your swimmers that you see all of them as potential winners.

Plateaus

All swimmers will not adapt to your training program at the same rate. Some won't be able to swim fast until they are fully rested, and others will often swim fast during the season. This can become a point of concern when it affects the confidence of your swimmers, so talk to them when this occurs and keep them focused on the end result.

It always inspires me to hear my swimmers respond with an emphatic yes when I ask if they believe they can reach their goals at the championship meet even when they are swimming slowly in a dual meet. The great competitors go on to tell me that they know their training times are on schedule and that they will remain on schedule during the peak preparation period.

A Two-Way Street

Swimmers must communicate with their coach. Ask what you can do better to improve as a swimmer. Your enthusiasm and desire to be a better swimmer can ignite your coach's interest in you.

As a coach, your swimmers must believe they can talk to you. They should be able to ask you questions and get some of the answers. You must provide time for those athletes who need to talk. This implies that the coach must also be able to listen. Almost all swimmers will doubt themselves sometimes, and talking to their coach can dispel those fears and restore their self-confidence, especially when they realize that their coach has total confidence in them. Your swimmers will train more effectively when you help them understand the goal of a particular training load, so always be prepared to answer their questions.

You are the resident expert for your swimmers. You must teach your swimmers to come to you first with their questions and concerns. I always tell my swimmers that if I want my car repaired, I don't go to my banker. I also try to convey that I don't have all the answers.

I prefer to meet with my swimmers before or after workouts on the pool deck, because there both the swimmer and the coach are in their own environment. Problems can be resolved before they are blown out of proportion. I recommend that most team meetings be held before practice, and I prefer to have the individual swimmer meetings after practice. Your office can be reserved for special individual meetings.

Success depends on the coach's ability to communicate effectively with his or her team members.

In the Pool

A large part of swimmer–coach communication actually occurs in the water. Because it can be difficult to hear, get the athletes' attention and make eye contact. Keep it short and simple. Communication may be either a hand signal on their technique or even an enthusiastic "Right on!" during a hard training set. The important thing is to make your swimmers believe you are watching and evaluating them all the time they are swimming.

When coaching I place myself at different positions around the pool: the ends, the sides, on a high stepladder over the pool, and sometimes in the pool. I think all your swimmers should believe you are watching them during each training session. Former world-record holder Mike Troy stated that when he swam

for Doc Counsilman at Indiana, he believed Doc was always watching him while he was training. All the other team members also believed Doc was watching them.

In the Pool Area, Out of the Water

Team meetings are usually best when there are the fewest distractions. A classroom with comfortable seats and desks is ideal, but the pool deck can be a practical and time-saving location. If the pool has another team, divers, or a class in it, eliminate as much distraction as possible. Pick a corner and have the team face you with a wall behind you.

Make eye contact with each swimmer. Don't talk to them when they are talking to each other. When you get their attention, talk to each swimmer. In your team meetings, encourage feedback and ask for questions.

The Surprise Question

In one training session several years ago, I had gone over the training program for that day on the blackboard and had asked my team if they had any questions. One of our team captains asked me why we were doing one particular hard training set; because it was an endurance set, he obviously didn't believe it was necessary for his 100-meter breaststroke event. My first response was to overreact and excuse him from that practice, but then I decided quickly and emphatically to give him and the team, who were in a state of mild shock, some short, quick, and meaningful reasons why we were doing that set.

Not only was the team captain a leader during the swim set, he did the set enthusiastically. He had a great training session. After practice he thanked me for explaining that particular set, and then he went on to say that I was right about doing it. I was happy that I chose to communicate on this occasion instead of overreacting.

Away From the Pool

Many communication opportunities occur on trips and at team social functions. You can sit and talk with team members during the meals and during the drive or flight on road trips. There are also long periods of time to talk at some of the full- or part-day swim competitions, or your swimmers may have an extended period of time between competitions. These are all excellent opportunities to increase the level of communication on your team.

At the Competition

Talking to your swimmers prior to competing will make your communication at competition more meaningful for them. Let your swimmers know what you expect from each of them in warm-up and cool-down. Tell them where to sit and what responsibilities they have while a teammate is competing.

I recommend talking briefly to your swimmers prior to each of their events and soon after they have completed an event. Before the race, a brief positive reinforcement of the race strategy and some attention to technique may be in order. The key is not to change the race plan at the last minute. At the conclusion of the race, share with your swimmers the positive aspects of the event, the race splits, and any improvements to be made for the next competition.

Whether it is necessary to relax your swimmers before their next race or necessary to excite them, it is your responsibility as coach to let your swimmers know that you are watching their swimming event very closely. Your comments after competition can be critical for your athletes' future success. Be positive but honest. Be concise yet brief, because there will be time for more details in the next training session.

Though communication should be positive, not every performance is always great. Sometimes we need to be told that we can do better. If a competitive performance is below expectation, it should be put in the proper perspective.

An Honest Answer

After a competitive race one of my team captains came to me for a postrace evaluation. He asked me, "How was it?" I told him his performance was bad, and then I told him why. He had taken the race out too slowly and placed himself in a deep hole. He didn't break out aggressively off the walls on his turns, and he had lost control of the race. I told him that this particular performance was below his level. He didn't like to hear the evaluation, but it was accurate.

A couple of weeks later, after the same event in another dual meet, he had performed very well. He then asked me the same question, and I told him that his performance was great and why. He then said something that I will never forget: "Coach, remember two weeks ago when you told me how bad my race had been? You were right. I didn't like hearing it, but thanks for being honest. It helped!"

Communication Tips With the Swimmer

- Stress the positive but be honest about the negative.
- Emphasize what they are doing right, and avoid emphasizing what they are doing wrong.
- Use praise to reinforce good performances.
- Correct the swimmer only when he or she can do better.
- Speak to every swimmer during every training session. An ignored swimmer is an unhappy swimmer.
- Coach at the swimmers' eye level or close to it. Kneel, crouch, or sit close to the swimmers whenever possible.
- Create pictures with your words: "arm out front like a spear."
- Be as specific as possible: "Finish the hand of the arm stroke here."
- Use words that are easy to understand.
- Use your body—arms, hands, shoulders, hips, and legs—to emphasize a point.
- Call your swimmers by name when speaking to them.
- Ask for feedback from the swimmer on technique. "How does it feel?"
- Concentrate on one point at a time.
- Be patient. If the swimmer hasn't learned, the teacher hasn't taught.
- Be short and to the point.

Too many words can cloud the picture you are trying to convey, and the message can get lost. One example of getting the message across with just a few words is attributed to Abraham Lincoln just before the end of the Civil War. "To: Lieut. Gen. Grant: General Sherman says that if the thing is pressed, Lee will surrender. Let the thing be pressed. A. Lincoln." Another example was when Winston Churchill gave a much anticipated speech to his former English prep school. He walked out, looked at the audience, and delivered his total speech, "Never! Never! Never! Never! Give up!" and then sat down. It may have been one of his most effective speeches.

COMMUNICATING WITH OTHERS

Besides your swimmers you need to communicate with others, because your success as a coach will be measured by your peers, colleagues, and various other members of the community. Your ability to converse with these groups can lead to good relationships and can help ensure a positive image for your team. Following is a discussion of the significant others with whom you will need to communicate to be a more effective coach.

Communicating With Officials

Swimming officials are most often volunteers in the truest sense of the word. They must take the time to study the rules and then go through a certification process—all to ensure that no swimmer attains an unfair advantage. I respect the officials, and I want my swimmers to do the same.

If one of my swimmers is disqualified, I want to know the reason for it. Whether I agree or disagree with the official, I must do so in a professional manner. I expect the official to explain the reason for disqualification to me, so that both my swimmer and I can avoid any future disqualification for the same reason. It is up to me as coach to teach my swimmers to compete within the rules.

In any negative officiating situation, ask for the rule interpretation in a nonthreatening manner. Accept the obvious infractions with a "thank you" to the officials. When you catch violations early in the season, you have time to eliminate them before the championship meet. If you disagree with the official's action, you can state your reasons but accept the ruling graciously.

You should insist that swimmers practice all of their strokes and turns according to the rules. If you permit your swimmers to do illegal turns in practice, then their chances of violating the turn rules in competition are greater. Pay special attention to your swimmers' starts, turns, and finishes; they are critical areas for possible disqualification in competition.

Communicating With Assistants

Communication with your assistant coaches is essential. In high school and college swimming, the assistant and the head coach will most often be on the deck at the same time; however, in club swimming, this is less often the case. Sometimes the assistant will even be at a different pool than the head coach.

Coaches' meetings are necessary and should be regularly scheduled, with weekly meetings the ideal and monthly the minimum. All coaches must know their responsibilities; they must understand the training program, they must be headed in the same direction, and they must understand the basic technique drills for the week.

I prefer meeting away from the pool, usually a dinner meeting where everyone is more relaxed and there's time for some social interaction. Coaches should have the time to present their views on how to improve the program. Coaches can also report on the progress of their swimmers. I make copies for my assistants of any new coaching materials I acquire, so they have as much information as possible.

Always make your assistants feel comfortable with providing their input at meetings. Give them ownership in the team by delegating responsibility to them in the form of coaching assignments. The more responsibility you give them, the greater their stake in the team's success. As a result, they will feel free to offer suggestions on how to improve the program.

Communicating With Other Coaches

You can learn a great deal from other coaches by keeping the lines of communication open. This is my philosophy: The more willing you are to share your ideas, the more likely other coaches will want to share theirs with you. With such an open-minded view, you will always have a steady source of information available to you.

The high school coach and the club coach of a particular swimmer must communicate, because when both coaches work together to bring the best of both programs to the athlete, they provide the swimmer with the best chance for success. When one of my Tacoma Swim Club members is on a high school team, I call or visit the coach. This policy is a win–win situation for the swimmer and for the coaches, because the swimmer's chances of improving are better, and the high school coach is more apt to refer new swimmers to the club coach.

Communicating With Parents

Parents are the most willing and anxious group of people to help their young athletes succeed. They receive too little information about their role as supporters of their athletes. It is your responsibility to guide the parents toward cooperating with your program. When you consistently communicate your philosophy and beliefs through your words and actions, then they can become the philosophy and beliefs of the swimmers' parents. This can result in the best environmental situation for your team members.

Whether you are a high school coach, a college coach, or a club coach, parents are part of the team. Usually, however, the younger your team members, the more important their parents are. For example, if the swimmer is too young to drive, then she or he must depend on a parent for transportation. Though the importance of parental involvement varies with the athlete's age, parents remain a vital part of any successful program.

I always try to have a parent–swimmer meeting at the start of each season. I go over the competition schedule, and I invite them to attend every possible swim meet. Then I explain how much time and work are involved in our program. I ask for their help in the "hidden training"—sleep, rest, and nutrition, because for the most part, parents can see better how well the athletes take care of themselves. Then I give the parents a prepared information sheet that contains the most up-to-date, scientific nutritional recommendations for athletes.

Finally, I ask the parents to love their children unconditionally and to be patient with them when evaluating their progress during the season. I then leave them with the assurance that my door is always open to them.

Follow-up socials are usually held sometime during the season and at the awards banquet at the season's end. A monthly newsletter is sent to all club members on our team, detailing most results, special events, a monthly calendar, and coming meets. I try to write a column almost every month, sharing my philosophy and my beliefs with club members.

Communicating With the School Faculty

I coached high school swimming for more than 30 years, and I have coached club swimming almost 50 years. High school swimming differs from club swimming, because it is an extension of the school's academic program. A high school swim

team must earn the respect of its faculty and its school administrators, and no one is in a better position to make this happen than the coach. You can support teachers when necessary by setting high eligibility requirements for your swimmers in academic achievement and classroom citizenship. I wanted the faculty members of my high school to support our team, because I knew that every teacher who recognized the accomplishments of one of my swimmers contributed to the potential success of the team.

I sought support from faculty members by requesting that they inform me if any swim team members fell behind in one of their classes. Any swimmer who was in academic trouble in any class was also at risk on the swim team for that period of time, and when it proved necessary, an athlete was denied the privilege to travel or to participate in competition and even in some cases was barred from our training sessions. I also informed faculty members that I expected my swimmers to be good citizens in their classes.

Setting such high standards earned for our team the respect of our school faculty and administrators. Many of the best teachers in our high school attended our major competitive meets and, when they returned to class, often praised our swimmers' performances.

In fact, some of the greatest support we ever received was from our faculty. Our bleachers, acoustical tile, and other equipment were provided by faculty members of our high school; our faculty presented water shows to students and parents over at least three years. The faculty did skits in and out of the water to raise money for special pool projects. It was great fun for all of us. The celebration party we had after the show each year also contributed to our school morale, creating a closer faculty and administration, as well as benefiting our swim team.

Communicating With the Student Body

The student body needs to be proud of the high school swim team. A winning tradition helps, but it will not stand forever by itself. There are many ways to cultivate student body support. For example, in our first years I gave bonus points to those students in my physical education classes who attended swim meets. Building attendance at the competition was the first step to attracting even more people. We built one meet, the Ram Relays, held every year just after Christmas, into a yearly tradition by having sales contests for our swim team members, with prizes for those selling the most Ram Relays tickets. The school pep band played to turn-away crowds almost every year that we had our contests.

In my first year of high school coaching, the school yearbook had one page for the swim team. By lobbying the student editors and the faculty advisor, we brought the yearbook section on the swim team to eight pages within a few years.

Then, there was that student reporter who was responsible for covering swimming in the school newspaper. That reporter got the red carpet treatment from this swim coach. The Wilson High School swim team was all over the sports page of the school newspaper in every possible issue.

Former Wilson students who were not swim team members still approach me in the community and compliment our great Wilson swim teams. Such student body pride helped keep swimming important in our high school.

Communicating With the Media

The media is your swim team's link to the community. Will Rogers once said that all that he knew he read in the newspapers. Today you can add radio and television to that. You can have the best program in swimming, but unless you get media support, very few members of your community will know about it.

During my first years of coaching, I had to build media support by hand delivering the results of our swim meets to the sports department of our local newspaper. Though my deliveries were usually in the evening and never convenient for me, I became acquainted with each of the sports reporters and the sports editor. My relationship with the editors really helped as we built a winning tradition. When our first swimmer competed in the

Olympics, the local newspaper sent a sportswriter to cover the event.

In 1968, our Tacoma Swim Club placed a swimmer, Kaye Hall, on the U.S. Olympic Team. She was also a Wilson High School student. She won the 100-meter backstroke event in Mexico City. Her world record, two gold medals, and one bronze medal assured Tacoma swimming programs of strong media attention for many years to come.

A Night Call

I still remember being awakened in the middle of the night in Mexico City by a telephone call from a Tacoma city official after Kaye Hall's Olympic victory. He was in charge of a planned media event, the homecoming celebration of Kaye's return to Tacoma. Suddenly, our swimming success was receiving media attention, and I couldn't help but reflect on those years of my personally handing our swim meet results to the local newspaper.

Acquiring the cooperation of your local media

- Consider the media to be a top priority after the meet. Call, or hand deliver, your meet results to local radio, television, and newspapers as soon as possible after the meet. Be prepared to deliver some good quotes and possibly have a very successful swimmer available for comments.

- Know your media deadlines and be sure to meet them. If you are on the road, phone in meet results before returning home, because a day late won't make it.

- Call whether you win or lose; it will help establish and build your credibility.

- Understand a newspaper's space and time restraints and be aware of slow news days. If basketball or football fill the sports pages on Saturdays and Sundays, but the paper runs features on

Thursdays, you have a better chance of getting your story in on the slower day.

- Find a kid on your team with a great human interest story, like overcoming some sort of handicap, achieving a high academic record, or excelling in another area.
- Look for media outlets that feature "athletes of the week" and find out how to get your athletes considered for the honor.
- About four or five days before a swim meet, provide a sportswriter who covers swimming with details of the coming meet. You may just hit the right moment for additional coverage.

BENEFITS OF A SUPPORTIVE COMMUNITY

The pride of our Wilson High School alumni became a positive factor in our community. In addition to school pride, the success of our Wilson High School swim teams and the national and international attention of our Tacoma Swim Club swimmers did much to communicate positive values to our community. For example, our Wilson High School swim team received two Washington State Senate Commendations at the state capitol, and both our high school and club swimmers received numerous commendations at the county, city, and school district levels.

While our community honored us, we reached out to others. Tacoma Swim Club hosted swim teams from Germany, Norway, England, Hong Kong, Japan, Philippines, and Belgium. Newspaper articles of these exchanges brought the program to the attention of our community.

The benefits of communicating with your community, through either actions or words, are many. For example, when we approached organizations and individuals in our community with projects to benefit swimming in Tacoma, we were successful. Our community aided in the purchase of an automatic timing system for our 10-lane pool in the Metropolitan Park District of Tacoma and also helped raise money for the Tacoma Swim Club to travel to international competitions and exchanges.

SUMMARY

1. Effective communication is vital to a swim team's success. This is the X factor in coaching.
2. Your style of motivation may change to fit the needs of the occasion or of the swimmer.
3. Enthusiasm is essential to communicating effectively.
4. Communication is a two-way street. Swimmers must feel they can come to the coach, so keep the door open to all.
5. Effective communication anticipates problems and eliminates any potential problems.
6. Communication in the pool is best when short and to the point.
7. Swimmers have to believe the coach is always watching and evaluating them.
8. Make eye contact whenever possible.
9. Recognize the opportunities to communicate: team trips, dinners, and the like.
10. Talk to your swimmers both as a team and as individuals, according to need.
11. Be positive but be honest!
12. Talk to the swimmers before, during, and after the competition to help them maintain focus.
13. Communicate with everyone who can help: parents, faculty, media, and the students.
14. Build effective communication through the positive accomplishments of your team.

Chapter 3

MOTIVATING SWIMMERS

Swimmer motivation requires a long-range approach. You must have a goal-oriented program that focuses on the long-term objectives of training, at minimum for a period of a complete season. There is a general trend to swim faster now and to make the daily training easier, and when this attitude prevails it adversely affects performance levels. Sell long-range toughness to your swimmers.

Swimming is an individual sport and it is also a team sport. It is best when the team aspect is emphasized. This has been proven time and again and was a major factor in the success of the USA Swim Team at the Sydney Olympic Games. At the high school and college levels, swimming becomes much more team-oriented, because the points that each swimmer scores contribute to team victories. It is easier to motivate swimmers when every swimmer commits to the team goals, and the most successful coaches understand and use this fact.

However, motivating swimmers as part of a team often presents challenges not found in other sports. The training period necessary for peak condition is extensive. Preparation is essential, and swimming fast through the preparation period to reach the championship meets is often difficult. That's why swimmers, perhaps more than any other athletes, need meaning, motivation, and fun in order to persist, and it's our responsibility as coaches to help them find these necessary elements.

In chapter 2, I stated that communication and motivation are intertwined. Good communication results in motivation. Motivation depends on some form of communication. The fact that each of us has two ears and only one mouth illustrates the importance of listening in communication.

WHAT MOTIVATION IS

If we can sustain intensive training and keep our focus on the purpose of that training, then we have the necessary motivation. When swimmers and coach excitedly come to each practice session and train with enthusiasm, then they have motivation. If this is the case in your program, don't worry about fixing it; it isn't broken.

Coach Motivation Versus Swimmer Motivation

Coach and swimmer motivation is like the chicken and the egg riddle: Which came first? I've always told my swimmers that they create enthusiasm, and that if they want their coach to be enthusiastic and excited at training and competition, then do something positive. Swim fast!

Swimming fast is a quick and effective answer to get your coach's attention. It will also encourage greater effort from all team members. Swimmers expect enthusiastic encouragement from their coach. The opposite is also true. Swimmers who are committed to improve their technical skills and training habits motivate their coach. Swimmers must also accept their motivation responsibility. Display your interest by your questions, actions, and enthusiasm. This is the best environment for both the swimmers and the coach.

I motivate my swimmers by urging them to generate some excitement. I get them thinking about their own responsibility to motivate themselves, but this doesn't let me off the hook; it just gives me another tool to encourage my swimmers.

How can you get motivated unless the swimmers are? I always say that motion creates emotion. As coach you shouldn't be like a plow horse pulling a buckboard of swimmers up a steep hill; rather, you should be like someone trying to hold onto the back end of a train's caboose that's under a full head of steam and going full speed downhill. Your swimmers stoke the engine with the fuel of their effort, and you do your best to keep the process going.

In other words, don't pull the motivation load by yourself. Inspire your swimmers, and you will be taken along for a most exciting journey. When they lack necessary motivation, recall the purpose of their efforts.

Developing Purpose

Purpose is the goal, the objective, the prize, and the direction. The greatest thrill swimmers can experience is to swim fast at the championship meet. No matter how much fun they have in the social and competitive events of a swim season, their fun is diminished by swimming slow at the championship meet, so prepare swimmers to do their best in the season finale. This is your purpose in training and you can use it throughout the season to keep practice exciting. There's nothing like looking back on a season of training culminated by a successful championship meet.

Pain and pleasure are often listed as prime motivators. What hurts in swimming and what is fun? A particular muscle may hurt for a very short time during a very intensive training set or even in a competitive swimming race. However, the greatest hurt is losing or giving a substandard performance. This pain can sometimes be long lasting. The most pleasure comes from winning and personal best performances. This can be a great motivator throughout the training preparation prior to the championship meet.

A Purposeful Answer

I give my swimmers questionnaires so they can provide feedback for the program. On one questionnaire I asked, "What is boring in our training program?" Most of the team looked for and found something that was boring for them in their program—long warm-ups, long kicking sets—but one very perceptive swimmer answered, "Nothing is boring in our training. Everything that we do has a purpose."

I received that questionnaire more than 25 years ago, and I have never forgotten it. Everything we do in training should be important, and it will be exciting when it has a purpose. My most recent team questionnaire asked, "What factors have the greatest influence on your successful performances?" The swimmers were to rate those factors on a scale of one to three. I provided the following selections: water training effort, dry land training effort, nutrition/rest/sleep, attendance, consistency, and any other category of their choice. The best answer that I received was that they were all number 1, that they were all important. That swimmer was able to see purpose in everything he was doing in his training.

Although you may have the best plan in the world, if your swimmers do not see the purpose of it, they won't be motivated, and you won't succeed. Making your swimmers aware of the reasons for your training regimen is necessary in any program.

It's easy to get excited about fast swimming, but it's important to remember that swimming speed is relative to each swimmer—a slow swim for one might be a fast swim for another. Recognize each swimmer's personal best practice and competition swims. Praise the successes and teach your swimmers to do likewise to their teammates. Recognition of swimmer achievements is vital. I like to recognize particular achievements by any of the team members in competition in a short meeting with the team, either after the meet or before the next day's competition or practice. It is important to acknowledge the swimmer's success shortly after the achievement. Remind your swimmers occasionally throughout the season why they are on the team—to swim fast—and where they are headed.

Developing a Sixth Sense

Knowing when a swimmer or your team needs special motivation is a sixth sense in coaching. Develop the ability to recognize when a swimmer or the team needs reviving. Change your training sessions when you sense they are becoming too routine. For example, if you're afraid your freestyle swimmer might become stale, change him or her to individual-medley training sets for a period of time, or hold a team meeting to inspire your swimmers.

A number of signals from swimmers indicate the need for motivation. If they act lethargic on arrival, sit with their heads drooped, get into the water too slowly, disregard the assigned time interval, or act generally disinterested, then they are ready for a motivational transfusion.

Sources of Motivation

Swimmers haven't changed much in my 50 years of coaching. Every young athlete wants something—usually some special and personal success. An athlete's desire may be buried deep inside, and he or she may be afraid to admit it, but make no mistake; it is there someplace.

Stories and movies about someone overcoming adversity and attaining success or winning have always been popular. Everyone fantasizes about being successful, but the problem is that few athletes devote the effort required to achieve their dreams. Will they do what they have to do, day in and day out, to succeed? Will they stay motivated to train and to push themselves during those intensive water workouts? These are the questions you have to pose to your swimmers.

Personal Drive

Personal drive is the greatest source of motivation. All athletes have a background of habits already formed before they become a member of your team. Long before you have the opportunity to coach them, your prospective athletes are learning from their parents how to work hard and to be persistent. In many respects, great parents make great coaches, but you, the coach, have the opportunity to ignite that spark of personal drive in each athlete. By establishing goals with your swimmers, you can set their personal drive on fire.

Time Standards

Unlike my earlier years of coaching, time standards now exist for qualification to enter particular meets at almost all levels of swimming competition. This built-in goal-setting procedure has a great impact on swimmers. Every age-group swimmer knows the time necessary to move up one classification, and every coach knows the effect that these standards have on their swimmers' personal drive.

Swimmers' Development and Success

An athlete who achieves is a motivated athlete, so teach the basics and gradually move to higher competitive levels according to your athlete's development. Many small successes will motivate your swimmers and give them confidence, allowing them to persevere through setbacks.

Swimmers can also motivate themselves with their own individual successes. A swimmer who attains a goal usually wants to reach a new one at a higher level. Therefore, you have to acknowledge success in your swimmers, regardless of the level at which they are succeeding. Encouragement for a good practice or competition might be a pat on the back, a handshake, or just a "thumbs up," but you should do it soon after each success. In this way, you build your swimmers' confidence not only by recognizing their successes but also by reinforcing those correct techniques that yielded improvement. Thus, as your swimmers attain greater skills through correct practice, they become more confident in competition.

Swimmers have repeatedly indicated that they want recognition and feedback from the coach. In the latest questionnaire, we asked our national training group, which included at least two national champions, "What do you want from your coach, at competition and at training?" At the competition, the swimmers wanted the coach to be enthusiastic, to provide honest and positive encouragement, and to believe in them. During training, the swimmers wanted challenging workouts, with positive reinforcement and encouragement from the coach. This again points out the need for good communication skills.

Kenneth Blanchard and Robert Lorber describe this process completely in *Putting the One Minute Manager to Work* (Berkley Pub Group). "People who feel good about themselves produce good results" (1984, p. 17). When people do something good or right, praise them for the achievement. This is exactly what the swimmers were telling us in the previous paragraph. Blanchard and Lorber's book wasn't written for coaches, but the principles work in coaching. I recommend that all swim coaches read this book, and I refer to it again in chapter 7.

Success Builds Success

Our unbeaten record at Wilson High School stretched through 24 years. When our team first started that streak, I feared that the media was putting too much pressure on them, but as it turned out, I was wrong; the problem was mine. I had to become comfortable with the attention that went with winning almost all of the time. The best part was that it helped us avoid complacency. Our teams, and even our opponents, expected us to win.

EXTERNAL INFLUENCES

I have drawn some conclusions about external influences. Who motivates you most in training? Who motivates you most at competition? The questionnaire to our highest level athletes indicated that the swimmers took the greatest responsibility on themselves. They knew that each of them has the ultimate responsibility. However, the next greatest source of motivation is the athlete's teammates. Athletes are pushed to their training limits according to the effort and the encouragement of their teammates.

The coach also plays a strong role in testing the athlete's limits. The wise coach will promote an environment that uses the motivational potential of teammates. For example, you can arrange the lane assignments to best challenge the swimmers in each lane or place swimmers in head-to-head training on occasion. By increasing the level of competition among teammates, you encourage them to perform at their best.

"Hidden training," the sleep, rest, and nutrition of your young athletes, also plays an important role in motivation. My most recent questionnaire indicates that the responsibility is ultimately with the athlete. Swimmers recognize that coach and parents both play an important role here. A home with plentiful supplies of the proper foods and a reasonable curfew can make the difference between the success or failure of your swimmer. The successful coach educates swimmers' parents in this area.

MOTIVATIONAL TOOLS

Positive motivational quotations are excellent, for example, "Turkeys flock, and eagles soar," "Success isn't forever, and failure isn't fatal," and "Only perfect practice makes perfect." Such messages serve as constant reminders of the direction every team member should be headed. I used to pin poster-size motivational messages on the team bulletin board, changing the quotation every few days.

Fortune Cookie Motivation

One night at a Chinese restaurant I received, in my fortune cookie, the motivational message, "You are going on an important journey." It was just before the start of the high school season. I posted the fortune cookie message on the bulletin board. To my surprise, our team not only noticed it, but read it with great interest. Because it was smaller than the typical message, it had grabbed their attention.

This marked the beginning of many years of the Fortune Cookie Corner on our bulletin boards. I would rotate inspirational quotations reduced to the size of a fortune cookie message every few days. The idea grew. Team members submitted fortune-cookie-size quotations for the bulletin board. We had contests for the most motivational quotations each week and for the season. The team members voted on the winners themselves. The process itself became a motivational event, and it bonded our team together.

When we were going for our 24th consecutive state championship meet, fortune-cookie-size messages were all over the place, with the number 24 in nearly all of them. When I picked up the telephone, 24 would be under the receiver. When I opened the door, I might find 24 on the doorknob. I'd started this practice, but our team members had carried it through the season.

Books, tapes, articles, and illustrations can all have a role in motivation. I have played motivational audio- and videotapes with great success, and I copy and distribute articles to my team frequently.

However, because tapes take time away from training, you should use them infrequently or recommend that swimmers play them at home. Books, particularly chapters in books, and articles are also best given to swimmers to read on their own. Avoid using training time for anything other than training.

Speakers

Speakers are a very good motivational source. Our team members can relate to athletes who have gone through our program and have been successful. Some of these previous athletes were not fast, successful swimmers, but they did very well in their careers. All credited their career successes to their swimming experiences as a member of our team. Over the long run, such testimonials from previous swimmers in our program had the greatest impact. Successful swimmers or other athletes outside of your program are the next best choice for motivational speakers.

Adversity and Success

One of our former swimmers spoke to our club banquet on motivation. He had been a successful swimmer at Wilson High School, Tacoma Swim Club, and Princeton University. He talked about how his time in our program helped prepare him for handling adversity and achieving success outside of swimming.

He once had tried to make the Junior National Championship time standard in the 200-yard backstroke. On the final day of competition in the last available qualifying swim meet, he failed to make the standard in the prelims and in the finals, even when he took two more time trials after the meet was over. All of his swims were within a few hundreths of a second of qualifying. At the time one of his teammates told me that she felt very sorry for him. I told her to forget about the pity, that he would be tougher and more determined because of the experience—and he was. Later in his career he went on to swim in both the Junior and Senior National Championship meets, as well as the National Collegiate Athletic Association (NCAA) Division I Championship meet.

About six years later, he was rejected by all the medical schools to which he had applied for admission. He was faced with the decision to change his professional goals or to try again. He returned to school for additional science courses, and two years later he was accepted to medical school. At the writing of this book, he has completed medical school plus eight years of residency and is now a noted pediatric neurosurgeon. He also teaches in the Columbia University Medical School Residency Program. He credits his persistence and ability to handle adversity to his swimming experience.

Inspirational Events and Experiences

I use experiences such as the one of our neurosurgeon in my own team meetings. However, whenever possible, I use recent experiences that involve the present team members, because their interest level is higher when the story relates to or involves one of them.

THE POWER OF GOALS

Successful coaches and swimmers have both a pressing need to excel and a clear vision of where they are going and what they are doing. Goals are the motivational foundation of a winning season. You and your swimmers must have real, vivid, living goals that will keep you going through every temporary setback that might occur.

At our first Senior National Championship, our team of four swimmers failed to qualify for any final events; all of them ended near or at the bottom. It was a humiliating experience for me, having been a consistent winner in our state and regional competitions, but it made me more determined than ever to reach our goals of scoring and winning at the national championship. I had to restate and reaffirm my goals that my swimmers would go beyond just qualifying to enter the championship meet. I was determined to qualify swimmers, but I needed to go the additional step and place them at the meet. It would take better organization, planning, effort, and determination. We did just that and had a national champion the next year.

Goals keep everyone on target. In my case, goals provide direction; they commit me to whatever is necessary to achieve success. Goals provided me the energy and drive to accomplish the task of producing great swimmers.

The key to goal setting is this: Your objectives must be high enough to excite you, yet not so high that you cannot vividly imagine achieving them. You should be comfortable with and confident in your goals and able to see yourself attaining them, even though they are just out of reach for now.

Jim Wood, coach of the Berkeley Aquatic Club in Berkeley Heights, New Jersey, states it simply and to the point with his swimmers. "Goals need to have three particular components: (1) They must be specific, (2) they must be exciting, and (3) they must be believable." His swimmers write their goals in the present tense and positively stated. This covers the essential elements in goal setting.

Setting Team Goals

As coach you must realistically assess the team's opportunities for the coming season. In high school and college swimming, you may strive for the highest possible team finish at the league, state, or national championship. In club swimming, team placement in a championship meet might be a possible goal, or you might hope to qualify and place a specific number of swimmers for one of the championship meets.

Objectives must be high enough to excite you, yet not so high that you cannot vividly imagine achieving them.

Once your goals are established, both you and your team have to agree that those goals are reachable and worthy of your best efforts. Your swimmers must believe that they are an important part of determining the team goals. Great teams are made up of ordinary people who have given an extraordinary effort to accomplish their goals.

The Big Goal—Number 24

In my final year of coaching high school swimming, I had a typical preseason meeting with the members of the team. We listed our dual meet competition and our championship meet competition and discussed the benefits of a full and complete season of training. We agreed that winning the state championship had to be our primary goal.

Our plan was to use every meet as preparation to win our 24th consecutive state championship title. The team also felt pressure to maintain an unbeaten record through our dual meets as we had done over those 24 years, but that was secondary to another title.

We agreed we would train through all dual and district meets prior to the state meet. This meant training the day of and usually after each competition leading up to state. Our team knew that one of the dual meets would be very difficult to win, but we decided that if we rested for that meet, it would affect our state meet. And so we competed, losing a close dual meet and ending our unbeaten record to an out-of-state team, David Douglas High School of Gresham, Oregon.

However, we were not distracted by this loss. We went on to swim one of our best ever state championship meets. Every swimmer who went to the state meet from that team placed in the top six in their individual events, breaking several state and school records in the process. We won our 24th consecutive title, thanks in part to our preseason decision to focus on our primary goal regardless of setbacks.

Goal-Setting Principles

Setting performance standards is the first step toward achievement, so you want your athletes to use goal-setting methods that have worked time and again. These are the principles I emphasize to my swimmers:

- State your goal positively.
- Be specific and lock yourself in to the end result.
- Avoid setting time limits on some goals, so you can have long-range goals that do not have a time limit and short-range ones that do have a time limit.
- Keep personal goals to yourself or limit the people with whom you share them to only those who can help you attain your goals. You should always know the objectives of your athletes, so you can relate their training to attainment of their goals. Race-pace swims are one example, because these must relate to the goal time.
- Reset your goals as you approach or attain the present one.

My first organized thoughts on goal setting came through a business friend of mine more than three decades ago. He loaned me an Earl Nightingale record called "The Strangest Secret." Basically, Nightingale stated that people with goals succeed because they know where they are going. The key to success is believing. Believe and you will succeed.

Earl Nightingale outlined these steps for setting goals. Picture a goal in your mind, and think of it in a relaxed way. Write it down on a card and carry it with you for 30 days. Look at it several times a day. Stop thinking all negative thoughts about the goal, replacing them with positive ones. Take control for 30 days, confident that you can achieve the goal, and it will become a reality. I still use these concepts as the basics for my goal setting.

Setting Swimmer Goals

Some coaches set goals for their swimmers; I usually don't. I can get the wheels turning in their heads, but I can't determine what they will commit to do. The goal has to come from the swimmer to receive commitment. In other words, I can suggest but they must invest.

For example, I gave my swimmers a chart that listed the American and the National High School record for all swimming events and the current qualifying times necessary to swim at the Senior National Championships, Sectional Championships, state high school championship, and league or district championship meets. I also would include the necessary time standards for All American selection and the current state and varsity records. I would list the top six swimming times in each event, as well as the consolation finals of the previous year's state championship. I gave them the chart each year and then let them use it to build their own dreams.

Dreams Transformed Into Goals

Early in the preseason I talked about dreams and about goals. I would have my swimmers list about 10 or more things that they wanted to accomplish in the coming season. I then had them list those things in measurable and specific terms; for example, "I want to win the state championship in the 100-yard freestyle," or "I want to swim 46.80 in the 100-yard freestyle."

My next step was to have them prioritize the top two or three goals from their list. These were to be the most important goals for the swimmers, and they would write them in their logbooks, on their study lamps, on the bathroom mirror, or inside their locker

doors. The swimmers would carry these goals, see them, and dream about them frequently for a few weeks, and when they truly believed that they could attain their stated goals, they would meet with me, and I would write their goals in my personal training logbook.

How will your reach your goals? What will be necessary in training, technical skills, and experience to attain your goals? This step should be part of your goal-setting process.

Reasons Lead to Commitment

The primary step in goal setting is to have the swimmers list their reasons for wanting to reach their objectives. It took me many years to add this step to our goal-setting process, but when I finally did, it resulted in greater commitment by the athletes, as these examples indicate: "I want my parents to be very proud of me," "I want to feel good about the results of my own hard work," and finally, "I want to attain a college scholarship time."

Reasons bring meaning to the pursuit of a worthy purpose. Purpose is a mixture of feelings, including a sense of usefulness, a connection with others, and a sense that we are doing something necessary and worthwhile. The reasons for a goal are often more important than the goal itself, because reasons lead to commitment. Swimmers who can visualize how it feels to win, to make the finals, or to do their best time are often highly motivated. However, seeing the time and the place on the scoreboard, hearing the cheering crowd, and receiving the congratulations of their teammates can also lead swimmers to greater commitment.

Gold, Not Bronze

Brian Goodel, Olympic gold medalist and world record holder, told me that during his training sessions leading up to the 1976 Olympic Games, he pretended to be in the Olympics. He would always see himself on the top step of the award stand, receiving the gold medal around his neck. The United States flag would be raised, while the "Star Spangled Banner" played. These images motivated him during the long and hard training sessions preparing him for the 1,500-meter freestyle in the coming Olympic Games.

At the Olympic Games in Montreal, Brian was trailing two swimmers with 400 meters remaining in the race. He said he was tired and thought about how third place and a bronze medal were not so bad. But then his thoughts came immediately back to that image of winning the gold medal. That image of winning that had helped him during his training gave him the motivation and the determination to come from behind, win the event, and break the world record in the process.

Monitor the Process

I recommend meeting with your swimmers at the start of the season to initiate the goal-setting process and to record their goals. Reexamine their goals at midseason and again just before the championship meet. It may be necessary to adjust a goal because of an injury or illness. In most cases, swimmers will remain committed to their objectives. Monitor the training necessary to help your swimmers reach their aims. When you've locked their workout regimens into place, be a contributor, a teacher, and a cheerleader for the athletes.

Setting Coach Goals

Although most of us are in coaching for the right reasons, we need goals to provide direction and focus to our programs.

Most coaches take some kind of break, a few weeks or months, depending on whether they are in a school or club program—when they can discover that there are other things in life outside of coaching swimming. I tend to get a little lazy during these periods, but with specific goals, I can get back a strong work ethic for the next season. I visualize the team and myself achieving our goals, and I get excited about starting a new year.

An Example From Experience

The greatest test in setting my own goals came at the beginning of a new high school season just after my first Olympic Games experience. I was on the airplane returning from the Mexico City Olympics. It had been a long season of preparation for the Olympic trials and all of the other competitions leading into the Olympic Games. One of our team members, Kaye Hall, had just won two gold medals and one bronze and had set a new world record for the 100-meter backstroke.

Naturally, my spirits were higher than the 35,000 feet at which we were flying, but my body and mind were exhausted. I had just been through two years of preparation for the Olympic trials and the Olympic Games, and now I had to begin a new season of boys' high school swimming almost as soon as the plane landed. I began to write down a possible competitive meet lineup for the coming season, and I started to dream about what those particularly talented young boys could do before the end of their high school careers. I listed our team goals and what I thought each swimmer could do that year. I formed teaching plans and training objectives for that season. I believed we could win the state championship with this young team just in their first year of high school swimming, and I could picture it vividly as I flew home.

That airplane ride seemed very short. I became very excited about getting started again in a new season, and when that airplane landed in Seattle, I hit the ground running. Suddenly I was enthusiastic again, and I can remember the feeling even now after more than 30 years. That year we won our 10th consecutive boys' state championship, and two years later in those boys' senior year we won every event except the 50-yard freestyle at the state high school championship meet.

Results of Goals

Goal setting should be an exciting process, because it dares you to reach new personal horizons. Excitement also comes from the intensive training necessary to attain objectives and from their actual achievement. Establishing and seeking goals can give meaning to your coaching, to your team's effort, and to the swimmers' efforts in training and competition. Exploring your reasons for attaining goals helps provide your commitment and sustain your motivation. Furthermore, the benefits of this process carry over to all phases of the swimmers' lives. Setting goals enables anyone to be successful. This applies to school, on the job, in relationships, and throughout life.

I believe that the way we set goals was one of the reasons our swimmers did so well in school. Our swim team had the highest grade point average of all the athletic teams in our school almost every year. More than 95 percent of our swimmers went to college, and a very high percentage of those graduated. Great swimmers manage their time well and succeed both academically and in the pool.

Attaining and Sustaining Goals

After the athletes' goals are properly set, the focus of the total program shifts to reaching these goals. It is your job to effectively organize the athletes' training time. Your swimmers must feel that all activities scheduled for them will help them succeed.

Throughout training, the primary source of swimmers' motivation must come from within them, not from you. The swimmer has the power to choose how fast he or she will swim a particular training set as well as the ability to select the best send-off time he or she can attain on an appropriate training set.

As coach you can reward swimmers who attain goal times or take major steps toward those times in practice. Rewards help reinforce the swimmers' determination to succeed, and they keep the swimmers more highly motivated during training sets.

Persistence in the pursuit of goals is an important characteristic of successful swimmers, coaches, and teams. When the stress of a long swim season begins to lower your team's motivational intensity, you must recognize it and adjust your program accordingly.

Rewards

Rewards don't have to be of material or monetary value; the greatest rewards are usually the easiest to give. Meaningful attention from the coach is a great reward. When you look into the eyes of young athletes and express your recognition of their exceptional effort, you give them a significant reward. It can also be one of your finest moments in coaching.

The greatest reward I get from my swimmers is a simple thank you. The swimmer who approaches me after an intensive training session and says, "Thanks, coach, for a great workout," does more to motivate me than anything else in my coaching.

Recognition also means a lot to athletes. Recognize their efforts and try to keep it simple. I have also used a season-long point table as a reward. I detail this in chapter 12 under tips for making practices fun.

Build Leaders

"Leaders are made, not born. They are made by hard effort, which is the price all of us must pay to achieve any goal that is worthwhile." This quotation is attributed to Vince Lombardi.

The first person whom you lead is you. Good leaders commit to helping people win. This is the coach leadership role. If your swimmers are not performing well, step up to the mirror and take a good look at yourself. If someone fails, step up and accept some responsibility. Respond by giving quality support to your swimmers and meeting their needs. In order to keep leading, you must keep learning.

Everything rises and falls on leadership. Leadership develops from the inside out. After the National Championship Rose Bowl football game, the University of Miami coach was asked what was the key to the success of their

undefeated season. Was it talent, character, or something else? The unequivocal answer was that the key was the character of the team. This was just one of the many references that character is more important than talent.

What makes people want to follow a leader? It is the qualities of the individual person who is leading. Through your coaching, you are providing a great opportunity for your swimmers to acquire leadership qualities. Talent is a gift, but character is a choice. Leaders give hope; they share themselves. People enjoy leaders who are optimistic and excited about their commitment. The roadblocks to leadership include cynicism, pride, insecurity, moodiness, and perfectionism.

DISCIPLINE

There are fewer opportunities available for young people today to acquire good discipline. Athletics remains one of the best sources for learning discipline.

Discipline has many definitions, one of which involves exercising strict control to enforce obedience. Another type of discipline comes from encouraging the gradual development of self-control, orderly conduct, character, and new habits. My swim programs have always functioned best under this second form of discipline. Swim training requires self-control over an extended period of time, before the thrills of competition take place. In addition to training, your athletes must develop self-control in their personal and social habits. In other words, establish for your swimmers those standards of conduct that will contribute most to the success of your team. For example, you might make attendance in school a requirement for participation in competition. You should make passing grades the minimum requirement for participation. You should also establish policies regarding smoking, drinking alcohol, or using other recreational drugs.

However, team standards should also focus on the positive. Your swimmers' pride is best built on a solid foundation. Ask yourself, can this team be its best without standards? Great swimmers demonstrate their discipline by choosing to attend practice, train diligently, study hard in the classroom, and adhere to the team standards.

Disciplinary Action

It's your responsibility to step in when the athletes fail to govern themselves. You must be prepared to make some hard decisions. Whatever disciplinary actions you may take, make sure they're fair and consistent. Be willing to discipline your fastest swimmer to the same degree as you would your slowest.

Your best corrective discipline for an athlete should never be considered punishment; rather, it must be a learning experience. I never disciplined athletes in such a way that they could not return to the team at some point. I made it clear that their mistakes had necessitated the disciplinary measures. I also would tell them that we could put it all behind us and that they had the opportunity to be reinstated as a full team member again at some point in the future.

I have suspended athletes for the remainder of a given season when necessary for a major infraction, but I always allowed them the opportunity to return to the club or school team the next season. Whenever a suspension was necessary, it was because the infraction violated our team's written code of ethics.

Personally, I don't like too many rules; I prefer standards, because, unlike rules, which are often things to be broken, standards are something to be attained. Some standards are necessary if the swimmers are to develop a strong sense of team pride. I suspended athletes when necessary, but this was an infrequent exception.

The discipline I find most beneficial for athletes is acquired in small steps day by day. Developing perseverance, hard work, competitiveness, and resilience requires this gradual form of discipline.

My form of discipline has more to do with accomplishing the things that need to be done than it does with avoiding the things that violate team standards. Discipline comes through maintaining self-control and choosing to make the most of your competitive swimming experience. Don't leave home without it—discipline!

SUMMARY

1. Fast swimming always motivates.
2. The innate desire to succeed is the best foundation to build upon.
3. Personal drive is the greatest source of motivation.
4. Success can breed more successes.
5. Teammates are the major motivators in training.
6. The swimmer is the major motivator in competition.
7. Motivational quotations are valuable tools.
8. Speakers can play a major motivational role.
9. Goals motivate.
10. Goals provide direction and destination.
11. Reasons bring meaning to the pursuit of a goal and lead to commitment.
12. The goal-setting process must be monitored continually.
13. The coach must set personal goals.
14. Goals provide excitement in the swim program.
15. The greatest rewards are the easiest to give, such as meaningful attention.
16. Discipline is a major success factor in swimming.
17. Discipline should be built around team standards, not rules.

Chapter
4

BUILDING A SWIMMING PROGRAM

B uilding a swimming program will depend in large part on the type of program you coach. There are high school, collegiate, and club teams. Club swimming involves USA Swimming, YMCA teams, and others. High school and college teams have shorter seasons, limited by their respective governing bodies. Their student athletes are eligible to compete only during their scholastic or collegiate years. Masters swimming provides a lifetime of competitive opportunities.

Club swimming is long term and can be a lifelong program when it provides a masters program. Scholastic and collegiate athletes usually continue to swim for a club team during their high school and college years. In high school this usually means the swimmer competes for the club team, except for the length of the high school season. In some states the high school swimmer can compete for the club during the season, as long as it does not conflict with the high school schedule. In scholastic swimming, this varies from state to state because each athletic or activities association sets the rules. College swimmers may swim for their club while their college is not in session, usually in the summer. Unlike interscholastic programs, collegiate programs are governed by one national body. Presently, the NCAA with Divisions I, II, and III sets their rules. There is also a smaller National Association of Intercollegiate Athletics (NAIA) collegiate program.

Most of my high school coaching career included only three years of high school swimming for each athlete. In my final years at Wilson High School, I had the swimmers for four years.

Tacoma Swim Club was another story. I actually had some swimmers on the team for 20 years or more. Some competed through the age-group, high school, college (both undergraduate and graduate schools), and some postgraduate years.

The type of program will determine much of how you will need to build your program. In this chapter I'll explain what it takes to build and maintain different types of programs.

BUILDING A HIGH SCHOOL PROGRAM

A high school swim team will be better when you have a good base of swimmers who have competed in club age-group swimming, but you must also take advantage of the many good athletes already in school who have not had previous competitive swimming experience. All of my successful high school teams included just such a mix of swimmers.

Recruiting Swimmers

Swimming is usually not a school-sponsored sport for elementary and middle school students. The best athletes in the school may have been playing other sports in elementary and middle school, so you must do more than just announce that the swimming team will begin practice on a specific date.

When I was a business education teacher, I traded teaching stations with the physical education teacher for one or two days in order to test the advanced swimmers for 50 yards of crawl, breaststroke, butterfly, and backstroke. These advanced swimmers were always our best source of potential competitors.

When I became a physical education teacher, I placed the students into groups according to their tested swimming ability. The advanced swimmers remained together as a unit through each specialty of the physical education classes, and, most importantly, they swam together at the same time at the start of the school year for a specified number of weeks. This gave me the opportunity to teach advanced swimming skills to them

for three to six weeks each semester. I then tested the advanced swimmers at the end of their swimming section for 50 yards in each of the four competitive strokes, thus providing me with a list of prospective swim team members. Finally, I met with each of the prospects and gave them a written invitation to join our swim team. We gained many new swimmers each year this way, many of whom became state champions and All Americans.

The most important sources of swimmers are the swim clubs and YMCA teams that are in your community. The swimmers who have had age-group competitive experience are usually the foundation of a successful high school team, because they already have some of the necessary skills and are usually the most receptive to an invitation to join your swim team. The Tacoma Swim Club, which I started in 1955, was the feeder system for my high school teams.

Team Levels

A high school swim team may have only varsity competition. If enough swimmers are on the team, and reserve competition is available, then reserve swim team experience should be offered. Wilson High School had a reserve swim team for many years, but competition from the other schools became scarcer.

Each swimmer's time for a particular event determines who swims the event in competition. Your fastest swimmers in each event would most often swim that event, especially in a closely contested swim meet. Instituting a program for each ability level is more important for training than it is for competition. The strongest and fastest swimmers can gain the most from having adequate pool time available. Also, the pool and deck space of each individual pool will determine the number of swimmers at each level. Your highest ability group must have the most pool time.

When necessary, I would group our team into three training levels depending on the ability and the number of swimmers. I actually had 65 boys on the Wilson High School team one year, and I was the only coach at that time. I ran this three-level training program to maximize the available space. I detail this practice in chapter 12.

Gaining Faculty and Administration Support

The support of your faculty and administration is often the result and not the cause of success in a swim program. If your swimmers are excellent students and citizens in school, they will receive faculty and administration support. This doesn't mean you can't take steps to encourage support. Invite the faculty to attend your swim meets, or ask them to be timers to get them involved. Sometimes it's best when the invitation to attend or to time meets comes from team members, because teachers, principals, and athletic directors are usually flattered that their attendance means so much to the swimmers.

I expected our high school swimmers to be leaders in school, and the faculty knew I would see to it that all team members met their academic requirements. Coaches need to check in and communicate with the teachers of their athletes. The team and I also served the school in areas outside of swimming, co-operating in many faculty and administration projects when we could. We sold tickets to various school activities, sold Christmas trees, raised funds through community dinners, and attended other athletic events as part of our volunteer school duties. All of these efforts produced for our swim team a special rapport with the faculty and administration.

One of our faculty members, to whom I gave some swim lessons, built our starting blocks, weight benches, and even our bleachers. A shop teacher who swam with me made some of our first hand paddles and our water polo goals. As I described in chapter 2, many of our faculty and administration acted in several of our annual water shows. I didn't believe that we could get teachers into bathing suits for swimming and then into costumes for the out-of-water skits, but we did. It raised school morale and was great fun for both students and faculty.

As our successes in the pool increased, our swim team and even our high school received more recognition. Our school principal always accompanied our team when we were recognized and honored with various citations by such groups as the Washington State Senate, the Pierce County Commissioners, and the Tacoma City Council. Many community service clubs also gave us special recognition each year. Placing several swimmers on the Olympic and other international swimming teams earned considerable community attention. Foreign teams and coaches coming to Tacoma for competition and training camps also helped us get noticed. All of this favorable attention, combined with our academic and volunteer efforts, secured great support from our high school faculty and administration.

Gaining Financial Support

The athletic budget is your base in a high school program, because it reflects the ability of your team to generate income, and we all know how difficult that can be in nonrevenue sports such as swimming.

Nevertheless, you should try to create at least one major meet that can generate income. Our income event was the Ram Relays during the winter holiday vacation, which became so successful for us that in some years it was named the homecoming event for our winter sports season. We ensured a large crowd by selling a substantial number of tickets during the several weeks leading up to the event.

Because our student council was another potential source of money, I encouraged some swimmers to run for positions on the council. The student council advisor was usually a friend of the swim team and a star performer in our faculty water show. When we needed to fund a pool project, our student council was a great ally.

For example, our student council funded the construction of bleachers to ensure adequate spectator seating. On another occasion, when the student council conducted a survey asking what school project was most needed that year, school officials were surprised that students voted for better acoustics for the swimming pool. The swim team's lobbying efforts paid off, because the student council appropriated enough money to start the project, about $800 toward the total cost of $10,000.

The faculty volunteered the labor to start the project. Because the issue had attracted so much attention and pressure, the school district finished the job. The high school budget is usually sufficient to cover at least the minimal requirements of travel, uniforms, and officials. Some supplemental fund-raising may be necessary to add something special for the team. Swim-a-thons, auctions, raffles, and special sales such as candy, Christmas trees, or old uniforms can bolster your funds.

BUILDING A CLUB PROGRAM

I will discuss some methods for building a club program that differ from those for building a high school program. Club swimming should be enhanced by receiving new swimmers each year from the high school program. This is reverse recruiting, getting the high school swimmers to continue in swimming throughout the year.

Recruiting Swimmers

Every year I coached, I recruited new swimmers successfully from our Wilson High School team for Tacoma Swim Club. These were swimmers who were new to competitive high school swimming and swimmers who had been dropout age-group swimmers. I wanted them to continue to improve, and the best method was to have them participate in a longer swim year. Their successful teammates who were already Tacoma Swim Club swimmers were the best recruiters.

In recruiting club swimmers, you should focus on younger swimmers. Swimmers who start swimming in high school are good candidates for a year-round swim club program. However, a successful swim club will need a continuous influx of younger swimmers. There is a lot of competition for young athletes in the wide variety of sports now available to them.

You need to sell these potential young athletes on the sport of swimming.

Community swimming classes are one of your best sources for finding new swimmers. You must recruit at every community pool that offers children's swim classes, from the local YMCA to your city park district program. You should also recruit in any summer swim leagues in your area.

Club Entry Levels

New club swimmers must be able to enter at some level of your club at any time during the year. Your club should have a swimming proficiency test for candidates, and those who pass can be placed into one of the team levels. Swimmers not yet able to pass the test should be placed into advanced swim classes somewhere in the community program and called back for a second test after an appropriate period of time.

I've found that a tiered system of ranking swimmers works best in training and goal setting. I had a three-level system for my age-group swimmers and two additional levels for my older and more advanced swimmers. This is an ability level grouping that challenges all swimmers without placing them in a program over their heads.

Each level should have a motivating title and create pride within that group. Specific objectives for each group and objective requirements for movement to the next higher level are a necessity. I leave the naming of the levels to you. Level I is the entry level for young, new swimmers and is designed to maintain excitement, energy, and a challenge to meet specific goals. Most of all, this level must be fun, so we emphasize games and relays at the practice sessions. For example, when swimmers are in the pool you can have them play water tag; out of the water, you can have such games as costume contests on Halloween.

A high percentage of your practice sessions must be devoted to instruction. Your swimmers need to be taught the basic skills, including the fundamental technique drills in all four competitive swim strokes, the streamlined or "torpedo" position off each wall, the basic turn skills, and streamlined kicking skills.

You should teach Level I swimmers the proper use of the pace clock. Swimmers need to know how to read it and how to maintain the designated spread (in seconds) between swimmers in their lane. Your swimmers must also develop the discipline of starting and finishing at the wall and adhering to the team-established circle patterns within a lane.

Level II is the intermediate step in your age-group program. Swimmers in this level do a bit more endurance training, some social events, and some team yells for competition. The relay games they participate in are longer and more continuous than those of the first level. Social events would include special pool activities on Halloween, Valentine's Day, and other holidays. Teach them team yells for the start of their competition at swim meets.

Your instruction of intermediate swimmers involves advanced turns and stroke drills, basic race strategies, an awareness and attention to stroke count, and some basic video analysis. Teach them how to pass swimmers in the lane and how to be the lead swimmer. Also instill in them the necessity of reporting to practice on time.

Level III would be the advanced competitive level in your age-group program. It is designed to be more goal oriented. Quality instruction remains critical at this level. Your swimmers must become very proficient in their technique in all four competitive strokes.

The prime event in this age group should be the 200 individual medley. You need to add more strength and flexibility training at this level. You should emphasize the importance of sleep, nutrition, and a healthy athletic lifestyle, and if you haven't already addressed it, discuss the detrimental effects of recreational drug use.

You'll need to add a level or two in order for your club to succeed beyond age-group swimming. Tacoma Swim Club has two additional levels for the senior team. The first of these is open to all swimmers who are within a specified number of seconds of the senior sectional time standards. The highest group, the national training group, is for those swimmers who have attained the sectional time standards or are within a specific number of seconds of a national time standard. Performance, not age, is the chief criterion for entry at this level.

Both groups train to improve their aerobic endurance levels and to prepare for their major event, the 400-yard individual medley. Having the same major event ensures that these swimmers will continue to train in all four competitive strokes. Here your primary job is quality control. You must emphasize good stroke technique and training habits to develop swimmers' speed and endurance, two important components at both training levels.

Your requirements for these levels may change slightly depending on the abilities of your current team members. You may need more levels or fewer, but this tiered system, which serves as the basis for our club program, permits movement toward more challenging levels for every team member.

Gaining Financial Support

Each club must raise the money required to meet their yearly budget, including the money necessary to rent pool time, pay the coaches, and cover the expenses of uniforms, travel, and competition.

I started Tacoma Swim Club on a shoestring. We didn't have a budget, and I volunteered to coach without pay. Fortunately, we had free pool space at the time. Within a couple of years, however, we had developed a parent booster club, which included a fund-raising chairperson, a treasurer, and other officers who would ensure our club's financial stability.

Monthly or quarterly swimmer fees usually form the base of the pyramid in club fund-raising. Other sources of revenue come from a variety of projects, such as swim meets, clinics, camps, and all of the methods previously listed. If you can recognize and accept your needs, you can find a person in your club with the talents to raise the necessary funds.

Community service clubs have been very helpful to us on occasion with special funding. In addition, the city park department, local YMCAs, schools, or other community organizations will often cooperate with the local swim club by providing pool time at a reasonable cost.

Alumni can also play a major role in fundraising. Several alumni have initiated donations to our club. We now receive a substantial amount each year in alumni donations.

Masters swimming is another good way to generate revenue and interest. Provide the time and space for the older swimmers who still compete. They are very often successful and influential community members who can afford to pay club fees and recognize the contribution that swimming made in their lives. They are the best sources of relating the needs of the swim team to the community. These goal-oriented masters swimmers can be your biggest boosters and fund-raisers.

Whenever we really wanted or needed something, we raised the money. One year we needed money to send our team on an exchange to Norway and Wales, so we conducted a fund-raiser that quickly earned $12,000. Another year we decided to purchase automatic timing for a 10-lane pool. Again, we raised about $12,000 through community service clubs and foundation grants.

A Goal to Europe

The year we raised $12,000 for our first trip to Europe, I set goals for every team member. Every swimmer who achieved the minimum dollar goal qualified for a two-day bus trip across the state. On the first day we competed in a swim meet, and on the second, we went to the World's Fair in Spokane. Two busloads totaling almost 100 members earned the trip, which was a great majority of our total team.

We have taken our club team to Europe three times for competition. We have also traveled to Mexico, Puerto Rico, and the Virgin Islands. All of these occasions required additional financial support, so don't get discouraged. When there is the will, there is a way. Don't use lack of funds as an excuse for having a second-rate swim club, because every team has the ability to attain the necessary financial support.

SIMILAR ISSUES

I have explored the major contrasts in high school and club swimming in this chapter, and now I would like to examine the similar areas of building a swimming program.

Establishing Fan Support

Fan support is easier to establish in a high school program than it is in a club. For one thing, a high school swim meet lasts about one and a half hours, and when you win in a high school setting, you're going to attract fans who have some association with the school and community, not just swimmers' parents. As the media announced our unbeaten high school record of 40, 50, 100, 200, and 300 meets, our fan attendance rose accordingly.

Star Attraction

When we had a potential American record holder at our high school, Kaye Hall, we would hold special events for her. Kaye was in high school before we had a competitive swim team for girls, so on occasion, we would have Kaye attempt to break the American record during a boys' high school swim meet. The proper sanctions and the necessary officials were arranged for the event at a time when it was within the rules. In these special swims, Kaye produced at least two American records, and again fans were showing up at our swim meets in increasing numbers.

A word of caution: Don't set up a special event like this unless you are quite certain that it can be done. Though you can gain credibility quickly by doing what you have set out to do, you can lose it even faster by failing. In my case, both Kaye and I were certain she would break the record, because she had almost done it in a regular practice session.

The more fans who show up for swimming meets the better. People attract people, and numbers attract greater numbers. When we first opened Wilson High School, I used to do anything to get fans in the bleachers. I gave students in my physical education classes extra credit for attending swim meets, and I brought in the pep band to play at the competition.

The pep band always helped create excitement. I suggest that you arrange pep buses to travel to your state meet, because when you fill pep buses and bring your pep band, you are assured of a strong fan base at the championship.

Creating fan support for club swimming is more challenging. Most meets are much longer and can go all day. Parents, relatives, and close friends make up most of the fan support at these meets. Their support is very important, and you must actively encourage it. Arranging a special seating section for your team's parents and friends will make it more of a social setting for them and will simultaneously focus the placement of your fan support.

In addition to the fans in attendance, media attention can generate fan support and provide a firm support base. However, remember that to get media attention, you have to make an effort to report swim meet results and to nurture relationships with local media members.

Making the Program Visible

Naturally, a winning program that produces individual state, American, World, and Olympic record holders is going to get attention. However, in my case, it didn't start out this way.

In my first year of coaching at Lincoln High School, I faced an uphill battle. The team had been on the losing end for several years. We needed to turn that around to attract any attention, so in our first year we moved up to third place at the state championship, and in our second we tied at state for first place.

We didn't talk about state records in those early years; instead, we went after what was attainable. We listed our school's varsity records and sought to break them. The record times were not fast for the most part, but the media nevertheless reported each record-breaking performance. This brought our swim team to the attention of our high school and gradually to our community.

Our second step to gain visibility was to defeat our cross-town rivals, who were the current state champions. When Lincoln High School, after only my second year of coaching, defeated Stadium High School of Tacoma in two very close dual meets, the entire community began to notice our swim program.

When Wilson High School was built, we had everything in place. Because it was a new school, almost every swim set a new varsity record. Then we started to break almost every state record, and we continued to do this year after year until I retired from coaching high school swimming. We also began an incredible unbeaten streak for all high school swim meets that lasted 24 years.

Our swimmers, both in club and in high school, broke national high school, American, Olympic, and world records. The high school team's list of All American swimmers continued to grow, whereas the Tacoma Swim Club swimmers were being recognized with world ranking more frequently. Visibility was never a problem after the first few years.

Instilling Pride in the Team

Pride comes from your swimmers' accepting the discipline necessary for team success. The discipline that builds this pride is reflected in the team's work ethic. Some bad habits may have to be replaced with good ones.

Successful swimming is the result of a great amount of hard work over an extended period of time. Swim team members must understand the necessary level of training intensity required for success. Next they must commit to attaining and maintaining that training level. Pride comes from the completion of every challenging training set. Pride also comes when their teammates challenge them to be faster in these training sets.

Pride comes from your swimmers accepting the discipline necessary for team success.

These swimmers will have meaningful pride and an elite level of physical fitness. Team pride results from individual pride. The team that works together, plays together, and competes together becomes like a family. When all members discover the pride that comes from committing to intensive training, then they are prepared to compete with confidence.

Cheering

When your swimmers cheer for one another, it builds pride and cohesiveness in the team. Your swimmers will produce an even greater effort when their teammates show their appreciation.

The results of cheering are obvious during swim-offs. When two or more swimmers have the same times for the last available position in the championship or consolation final, they "swim off" for that remaining available position. When the entire team stands at the sides and ends of the pool, cheering for their teammate to win, it has a great impact on the results of the race.

I always told my swimmers that I can't remember when one of our team members had ever lost a swim-off. I also tell them that I may have blocked out one or two misses, and I can't remember them. I expect them to reach down for something extra, and I expect every team member on the deck cheering for the desired result.

Winning Close Races

Winning close races also builds pride. Anytime we are close in a race, we want to be the toughest and strongest of all the swimmers coming to the finish line. Always recognize your swimmers who manage to beat an opponent in a close race, whether it's for first place, second, or third.

Excelling in Relays

One indication of team pride occurs when your swimmers' times are better in relays

than they are in individual events. Swimmers should be as good or better in a relay position than they are in their individual events for the same distance. Pride develops when all relay team members contribute to the effort at no less than their personal best individual swim.

Establishing Tradition

Finally, team pride comes from tradition. I posted an honor roll for every swimming event at our high school. It was printed on a kickboard bearing the name, the year, and the time listed for each swimmer who attained the specified honor roll time. We also listed all of our varsity and state records and our All Americans on special display boards.

Pride comes from swimming faster in both the prelims and finals. It comes from a great performance, be it winning or swimming a new personal best time. It is a necessary ingredient in personal success and is vital to team success. Our Wilson High School swimmers have said that it meant something special to compete in our team uniform. Such pride can be instilled in every athlete and team, and the opportunities to do it are always present. You and your athletes have to learn to recognize and to use every opportunity to build team pride.

SUMMARY

Building a swim program requires a well-organized plan with specific goals. In this chapter,

I explained the keys to successful high school and club swim programs.

1. Encourage swimmers to be good students and citizens, which will build faculty and administration support.
2. Encourage coaches and swimmers to serve their school outside of competition, to ensure the support of the faculty and administrators.
3. Recruit the best potential swimmers within your high school.
4. Establish an age-group swim team to provide a strong base of swimmers for your high school teams.
5. Provide training and competitive levels for all participants on your high school team.
6. Develop and encourage extensive fund-raising activities for your club swimming program.
7. Make your club team accessible to new swimmers at any time during the year, and provide enough levels to challenge all team members.
8. Incorporate fun, instruction, and discipline into your program.
9. Build fan support from your team's successes.
10. Develop team pride by helping your swimmers develop the discipline that comes with intensive work habits.
11. Use victories in a swim-off, relays, and close races to build team pride.

Part II

COACHING STROKE TECHNIQUE

Chapter 5

BASIC PRINCIPLES IN TEACHING STROKES

Coach Bill Sweetenham, the great Australian coach, stated that you must teach fundamentals first. "Fundamentals must be learned before training can take place. After the fundamentals, training must be on the basics, then train to train, then train to compete, and finally train to win."

The emphasis must be on correct technique. I list drills for each stroke in the coming chapters. Drills are designed to correct poor technique and to guide the swimmer into efficient stroking patterns. Drills are only effective when they are precisely taught, monitored closely, and done correctly; 100 percent correct is always the goal.

Swimming speed depends on several factors. Stroke length is the distance that the swimmer moves through the water from the entry of one arm to the next entry of that same arm or, as in butterfly and breaststroke, the distance reached by the simultaneous cycle of both arms. This is the distance the swimmer's body travels during any one arm cycle of swimming. Stroke frequency is the number of such cycles that would occur in one minute if the present stroke rate were continued. Stroke count is the number of arm strokes completed in each lap or length of the pool. Each of these factors can be objectively measured and provide a good reference to each swimmer's efficiency.

Swimming speed equals stroke length plus stroke rate, or stroke frequency. Many efforts are made to maximize the distance per stroke. This should be done in the early learning stages of the stroke. However, it is more important to optimize a swimmer's stroke length. Maximizing stroke length may decrease the swimmer's chances of winning. Optimizing stroke length gets the most distance per stroke with maximum efficiency. Optimize stroke length by applying good technique throughout the entire stroke.

To increase speed, the swimmer must be able to get more distance out of each stroke, optimizing each stroke and/or increasing the tempo or stroking rate. Most initial improvement will come from decreasing resistance and increasing the efficiency of each stroke. Much of your teaching will focus on increasing propulsion and decreasing resistance. It is more important for your swimmers first to learn to swim the strokes correctly before building stroke tempo.

Resistance is the result of the water acting against the swimmer's forward motion. The coach should focus first on reducing the resistance force because this requires less energy expenditure than increasing the propulsive force. When the greatest stroke efficiency is attained, then adding to the propulsive force will be effective.

OPTIMUM DISTANCE PER STROKE DRILLS

This is of prime consideration in determining the efficiency of each stroke and for each swimmer. I won't repeat this explanation in each of the four stroke chapters, so I'm presenting it once here in this chapter. Hereafter, I will refer to it only as "optimum distance per stroke drills" without further explanation for each of the coming stroke chapters. After you teach the skill drills in any of the four strokes, you can move on either to other drills or directly into those that maximize and then optimize the distance per stroke. Training sets should also come back to optimum distance per stroke drills.

"If you want to change something, then you must be able to measure it." I don't know when I heard this statement, but it is a fact. When you can measure a skill or performance, then you are in position to effect change. This should be a guiding principle in coaching.

Stroking efficiency is about counting strokes. Counting the number of strokes for one pool length is an easy and effective method to maximize the distance per stroke. Continuing to lower the number of strokes per length will maximize distance per stroke but will

eventually decrease the efficiency of the stroke. This should be one of the first steps in optimizing stroke efficiency.

The next step in optimizing the distance per stroke is to use a minimum number drill. I have used this drill since at least the 1970s, and I remember hearing it first from Coach Nort Thornton. In this drill, your athletes swim a given distance, for example, 50 yards. They count the number of strokes that they took and record their time. This will determine their minimum number. Minimum number swims are designed to equate your swimmers' race-pace split time with their most efficient number of strokes. For example, if your swimmer has a time of 28.5 for 50 yards and requires 31 strokes to complete the distance, then he or she would have a total number of 59.5 (28.5 + 31). If the same swimmer completes the 50 yards on a second attempt with a time of 28.2 but takes 32 strokes, then he or she would have a total number of 60.2. In this case, repeating 50 yards of swimming with a total number of 59.5 is the more efficient swim. As the swimmer progresses in proficiency, that minimum number should decrease on subsequent tests. This should equate to the current most efficient race pace at some point.

Coach Bill Sweetenham takes this drill and locks in a specific race pace quite objectively. Race pace can be determined by taking a personal best time for any event. If it is a 100-yard event, divide by 4. Determine the optimum or most efficient number of strokes it takes to complete a 25-yard swim at that race pace. If it is a 200-yard event, divide by 4 again and then determine the optimum number of strokes to swim 50 yards at that race pace. To improve on the personal best time speed, the swimmer can next begin to swim each section at the faster goal time and still maintain the optimum stroke count.

The stroke count for 50 yards at 200-yard race pace gives a measurement of swimming proficiency. As the distance increases, the swimmer would maintain the same stroke count for each 50 yards. For example, if it took 32 arm strokes for a 50-yard swim at 200-yard pace, then when the swimmer swims 100 yards at the same 200-yard pace, the stroke count of 32 should be maintained for the second 50 yards as in the first 50. This principle would be extended through 150 yards and finally the total 200 yards. The longer sections may have to be broken swims, but this helps to maintain the distance per stroke through the entire swim. The idea is to maintain quality with minimum effort in optimum distance per stroke drills.

Stroke rate is also a useful tool in measuring swimmer efficiency. It is measured by a stopwatch with a stroke rate function. Coordinating the optimum stroke rate that permits the optimum stroke count during race-pace swims can increase efficiency even more. Stroke count should be in place first before you use a stroke rate stopwatch.

Speed is measured for each swimmer by personal best times, efficiency is measured by counting strokes, and fitness is measured by heart rate. Using heart rate is an important tool in chapter 11 on training.

Speed and stroke tempo can come later. If the stroke length remains reasonably constant, speed is increased by increasing the stroke rate. However, as stroke rate increases, swimmers tend to have a marginal drop-off in stroke length. If the drop-off in stroke length doesn't keep pace with the increase in stroke rate, the swimming speed is reduced.

The speed that a swimmer attains is determined by two forces that must reach equilibrium. The propulsive force that a swimmer is able to generate against the water is one, and the other is the resistance force of the water acting against the swimmer's forward motion. The coach should focus first on reducing the resistance force because this requires less energy expenditure than increasing the propulsive force. When the greatest stroke efficiency is attained, then adding to the propulsive force will be effective.

SCULLING

Teaching swimmers to scull and use practice drills in sculling is a neglected area in coaching. Sculling enhances the swimmer's feel for the water, yet it can be a stroking fault in some instances. For example, in the crawl stroke, sculling on entry or on the catch wouldn't be correct. Chapter 7 is devoted to the crawl stroke.

I designed and manufactured special hand paddles that I believe are great aids in teaching and improving sculling skills. The Groover and Gripper (listed under swim aids in chapter 12) have grooves on the water side that assist in developing and accelerating sculling feel (see figure 5.1).

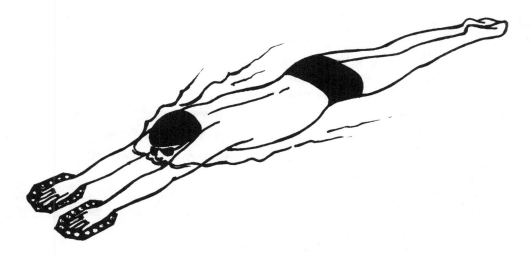

Figure 5.1   The arms extended sculling position using "Gripper" paddles. Maintain the paddles on or near the water surface in this drill. The chin is resting on the water, and the head is up. The legs are extended and don't kick.

The first sculling position that I teach is the front extended breaststroke position for sculling. Teach your swimmers to keep their hands high on the water, very close to the surface. Have them scull out by pitching their hands outward, or with the little finger higher than the thumb, and scull in by pitching their hands inward or with the thumb higher than the little finger. They should keep the scull continuous with pressure on the forearms.

Use all types of sculling positions, such as the midstroke position under the shoulders, also known as the windshield wiper position and the finish position. These can be done on the front and back positions. I also use synchronized swimming sculling with the swimmers on their backs, moving in a reverse direction, with their arms either overhead or at their sides. These skills are used to increase the feel of the hands on water for swimmers. Some swimmers seem to be born with this talent, but it can be improved in all swimmers through sculling drills.

DECREASING RESISTANCE

Resistance is the amount of water that your swimmer's body displaces while moving through the water. Basically, the more streamlined body will displace less water than its counterpart. The design of torpedoes proves that fact.

It isn't an accident that fast swimmers in international competition are more often built like race horses than plow horses. Very successful swimmers usually have tapered, streamlined bodies. Though height may not be critical, the best swimmers are tapered from the shoulders to the feet.

You may not be able to change your swimmers' basic body types, but you can help them develop more tapered bodies. Swimming requires long periods of stroking with both arms, and that alone helps to fill out the upper body and shoulders. Supplementary dry land training will also help in this regard. For the lower body, kicking drills will slim and firm the hips and thighs. Add good nutritional guidelines to your swimmers' daily energy intake, and they will develop more tapered bodies.

When you consider how a swimmer moves through water, you can easily see the advantages of a tapered body type. A streamlined body cuts a hole through the water at the head and shoulders, allowing the rest of the body to move through that hole without creating substantial new areas of water resistance at the stomach, hips, or thighs.

Also, water eddies cling to the swimmers' bodies as they move through the water, creating additional resistance. However, if swimmers are streamlined, they can keep their hips and legs within these eddies both vertically and laterally and avoid creating additional eddies and more resistance.

These principles of propulsion and resistance guide all matters of technique and all methods of teaching those techniques. In the coming chapters, I cover the necessary drills for teaching proper swim technique.

EMPHASIZE TEACHING

Take the time necessary to teach, especially early in the season and in the beginning years of each swimmer's career. Each year at Wilson High School, I devoted 30 to 45 minutes daily to teaching swim skills. This was usually done cross-pool in our diving section. I did the same thing in my club coaching.

Be persistent and relentless in your teaching. Expect the best and don't let up on your swimmers. Teach, teach, and teach!

Drills are only effective when they are precisely taught, monitored closely, and done correctly.

TEACHING GUIDELINES

I learned a lot about teaching and coaching swimming from a book that wasn't even a swimming book, *Putting the One Minute Manager to Work,* by Kenneth Blanchard and Robert Lorber. The basic principles of this book are as follows:

1. **Tell the person exactly what he or she did right.** I believe in strengthening positive mental pictures, so tell your swimmers what they are doing right, not what they are doing wrong. The negative mental picture created when swimmers see what they are doing wrong is not the best opportunity for positive change. On the other hand, if you praise swimmers when they do something positive, they feel good about themselves and what they are doing right. This is a valuable learning tool to use for your swimmers.

2. **Keep it short and simple.** This is called the KISS method. Swimmers can only focus on one or very few stroke tips at any given time, so keep your instructions short and simple for the best results. "Elbows up!" "Lengthen your reach!" "Finish your stroke!" All of these statements are concise and serve as positive examples of the KISS method.

Keep coming back to basics when teaching swim skills. Keep your program simple and easy to understand. The best swimmers do it naturally, almost without effort. All strokes flow best when we keep coming back to basics.

Breaking Out of a Plateau

When swimmers struggle in competition, back off from focusing on their time measurements. Put your stopwatch in your pocket and go back to some basic drills. Let your swimmers focus on the basics of good stroke technique by optimizing their distance per stroke.

This is what I did at state and national championship meets, even at the Olympic Games. To break out of a brief plateau, Kaye Hall trained almost totally on a few basic technique drills for about six days before

winning her Olympic gold medal and world record. Many Wilson High School swimmers scored at our state championship meet by doing the same type of technique training leading into their competition.

———————————

3. Never reprimand learners, because reprimands don't teach skills. You must be persistent in your teaching but patient with those willing to learn. Swimmers who are trying to acquire advanced skills must do so by learning, so treat them accordingly.

4. Watch your swimmers perform. Teach a skill and let your swimmers know you care by keeping an eye on them. Watching your swimmers makes them more aware of their need to perfect their skills.

5. Praise their progress or redirect their efforts to the task at hand. If they aren't ready to proceed, then have them go through the process again.

The following sequence should be repeated until your swimmers develop their skills adequately enough to progress to the next level:

1. Explain the swimming skill to be learned, and then have a competent swimmer demonstrate that skill.

2. Have your swimmers attempt the skill through practice.

3. Observe their performance and then either praise their progress or start all over again with the same teaching sequence.

The way in which *Putting the One Minute Manager to Work* provided a logical sequence to my teaching is just one example of how you can use articles and books directed toward other professions to help you in your coaching.

STROKE COACHING

A short time before Howard Firby (the Canadian National and Olympic coach) died, I attended a clinic in Canada where I heard him present suggestions for coaching strokes. I include many of his suggestions in this chapter before going into the specifics for each stroke in the next four chapters.

1. Begin with standard techniques. You can tailor the stroke to each individual's particular ability later.

2. Get the swimmer's timing and general movement correct before concerning yourself with exact or complex actions.

3. Develop the swimmer's skill first and the speed later.

4. Speak to every swimmer every session.

5. Address each swimmer by name.

6. Use common words and avoid academic expressions.

7. Sequence your details, permitting the learner to concentrate on one movement at a time.

8. Be concise and use word pictures, like, "Place your arms out front like a swordfish's sword."

9. Be specific. For example, use your own hand to illustrate a particular movement.

10. Start with something your swimmers already know and build from there.

11. Compliment and then correct.

12. Ask for feedback; have the swimmer teach the skill back to you.

13. Pick your demonstrators with care. The swimmer demonstrating can be just a notch above the learning group and still be very effective.

14. Be tolerant and patient. If the learner hasn't learned, the teacher hasn't taught.

15. Reward improvement.

16. Persist. Some swimmers need more reminding than others.

17. Avoid being "picky." Don't constantly interrupt swims to fix minor faults;

rather, note the problem and treat it at an opportune time.

18. Avoid distractions. Have your swimmers face you with their backs to any possible distractions. If you are sharing a pool with another team, move to the opposite end of that pool.

19. Coach at your swimmers' eye level whenever possible. Crouch or sit at the side of the pool or, when necessary, be in the water.

20. Use visual aids. Videotaping is one of the greatest advances in my own coaching career.

21. Use buddy coaching—swimmers coaching each other.

22. Make major changes early in the season for national level swimmers and constantly with lower levels.

23. Use stroke drills and progressions.

Learn by Teaching

I've used swimmers to teach their teammates certain skills necessary for good technique. The selected swimmer explains the skill and then demonstrates it either through a drill or in the swimming stroke. The swimmer-turned-teacher always does best when the spotlight is focused on him or her.

One of my own sons had a crossover four-beat kick in swimming the crawl. He did my demonstrations of kicking drills at several swimmer clinics for me and in the process picked up an effective six-beat crawl. Within two years he broke the national high school records in the 200- and 500-yard freestyle.

SUMMARY

1. Make technique and fundamentals your first teaching focus.

2. Teach technique by focusing on increasing propulsion and decreasing resistance.

3. Maximize distance per stroke and then optimize the distance per stroke.

4. Use sculling drills to improve the swimmer's feel of the water on the hand.

5. Take time to teach.

6. Tell your swimmers what they are doing right.

7. Keep it short and simple.

8. Never reprimand a learner.

9. Observe your swimmers' performance.

10. Praise your swimmers' progress or redirect them to the goal at hand.

Chapter 6

DOLPHIN OR BUTTERFLY KICK

The dolphin kick should be considered as a fifth stroke. It is used in both crawl and backstroke off the walls in starts and turns as well as throughout the butterfly stroke. For those reasons, I have chosen to include the dolphin kick in this chapter. This will be the reference chapter for the use of the dolphin or butterfly kick in the subsequent crawl, back, and butterfly chapters.

BODY POSITION

The underwater butterfly kick is most effective when the body is in a streamlined, torpedo position. It is most important that the swimmers understand the streamlined torpedo position (figure 6.1a). The arms are hyperextended overhead with the hands locked, one over the other (figure 6.1b). The head is down and the arms are pressed against the back of the ears. The eyes are looking downward when the swimmer is on his or her stomach. The back of the head and the spine are lined up in a "platform" position. This streamlined torpedo position must become a 100 percent correct habit in all four competitive strokes as well as for the dolphin kick. It must be an extremely efficient streamlined position to get the most speed off of the walls in the start and in the turns.

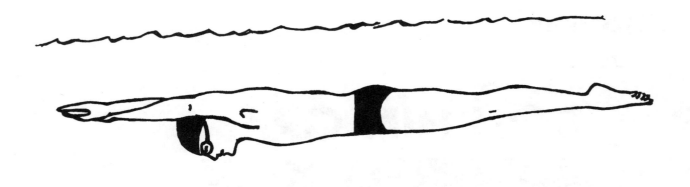

Figure 6.1a The torpedo position must have the back of the head and spine in line.

Figure 6.1b A below water head-on view of the torpedo position illustrates the overlapping of the hands.

THE KICK

The power kick should be performed from the hips through the legs, with the upper body from the waist to the head reasonably still and extended (figure 6.2). The upper body has a dolphin movement to provide the necessary rhythm, but that movement is minimal when compared with the movement from the hips down. The result should be a narrow, fast kick.

To keep the dolphin kick continuous and explosive, the most power should be generated from the hips through the feet. The dolphin kick when done with a single leg is the same as the crawl kick done one leg at a time. It is only in the combination of both legs that the kick is powerful. The depth of the kick will be in a slightly greater range than in crawl kicking because of the reaction of the simultaneous kicking of the legs.

The following drills have proved to be effective for this kicking skill.

KICKING DRILLS

Teeter Totter

A drill for beginners is to have them glide on the surface with their arms at their side and face in the water. Swimmers attempt the rhythm of the dolphin kick by pressing their chest down on the water slightly and then lifting their back in the same manner. The depth of the press and the lift of the back should be the same distance and at the same speed. Coach George Block, Alamo Area Aquatics and Aquatic Director for the San Antonio School District, calls this the "teeter totter" drill.

The progression in this drill is to gradually finish off the kick with a strong, fast leg action through the feet. This is similar to cracking a whip.

Figure 6.2   The bent leg position at the top of the dolphin kick (top) and the extended leg position (bottom).

One-Leg Flutter Kick to Dolphin

Novice swimmers should practice one-leg flutter kicking while holding the gutter. Next, they add kicking both legs simultaneously. Then they alternate one-leg kicking with each leg and then progress to simultaneous or dolphin kicking. The progression on this novice drill is to do the same procedure in a streamlined, torpedo position and also on the kickboard. This novice swimmer step puts the focus on the kick from the hips and not the upper body undulating movement.

Dolphin Kick With the Arms at the Side

The swimmer kicks two or three kicks on the surface and then two or three kicks underwater. The head leads in this drill and the kick is slower than desired. This helps the swimmer to attain the rhythm of the dolphin movement.

To keep the dolphin kick continuous and explosive, the most power should be generated from the hips through the feet.

Torpedo Underwater Kick

The swimmer kicks short, fast bursts underwater in a streamlined position. It's best to do these across the deeper end of the pool or in a diving well where the water isn't too shallow. Distances of 10 to 15 yards are very effective, and timing or racing with other team members provides increased incentive to improve this kick. Just staying underwater for this short distance is usually a motivating factor for beginning competitive swimmers, who have to kick fast in order to surface and breathe sooner. Novice swimmers can have underwater kicking distances shorter than 10 yards, perhaps only three or four fast kicks before surfacing. Short swim fins and the smaller monofin like the "shooter" are excel-

lent training tools for the underwater butterfly kick. The short cross-pool kick drills won't work with fins because the distance is too short for the speed generated with fins. The swimmer should perform the fin drills in the main pool over 15 yards or more.

The underwater kicking drills should be done first on the stomach. After attaining some skill, swimmers should next do these drills on each side and on the back. The back dolphin kick is very beneficial in learning an efficient dolphin kick. As the swimmer advances in technique, he or she should practice this drill with the arms crossed in front of the head in all positions: front, sides, and back.

Vertical Kicking

Vertical kicking with the arms extended overhead in deep water is an effective drill when used in short bursts of 10 or more seconds. The fin drills can also be used in the vertical kicking sets. Swimmers can advance to holding weights overhead to increase the challenge.

Bob Bowman, coach of the North Baltimore Aquatic Club, recommends that advanced swimmers do vertical kicking with weights to build strength, foot speed, and power.

Rockets

Bob Bowman also recommends "rockets." The swimmers submerge to the bottom of the pool, drive off the bottom in a streamlined torpedo position, and kick as many body dolphin kicks as possible. They attempt to hold that streamlined position with the body out of the water to the hip line for as long as possible. This drill is also used by Bob in repeat sets, with the swimmer holding a 10-pound diving brick overhead.

Back Dolphin

This drill involves surface dolphin kicking with the arms extended in the torpedo position on the back. Swimmers can practice this drill with fins and with the shooter monofin.

Front Dolphin, Hands Back

This drill involves surface dolphin kick on the stomach. The swimmer locks the hands behind the back, keeping the head out of the water with the chin resting on the water. This drill forces a continuous leg action to keep the face clear of the water. Swimmers can practice this drill with fins and with the shooter monofin.

Backstroke Flag Reach

This drill is a variation of rockets. To improve speed and efficiency, swimmers kick with fins, after pushing from the bottom of the diving well, in an extended torpedo position attempting to touch the backstroke flags on the kick. When your swimmers get good enough to reach the flags with fins, have them try to duplicate the drill without fins.

Dolphin or butterfly kicking drills should be performed at a fast, power-kicking speed. Swimmers should avoid a slow, lazy kick; for that reason, they should use the kickboard sparingly. The kickboard can be used in sets requiring speed and effort. This will keep the kick fast, continuous, and explosive.

Coach Bob Miller, Tucson Jewish Community Center in Arizona, offers this dolphin kicking set for improving the kick, breath holding, and streamlining. It includes a portion of the butterfly stroke as well, but the kick is the dominating factor in this set. The set consists of 20 × 50 yards on 45, 50, or 55 seconds depending on the swimmers' ability levels.

The swimmer pushes off underwater on the back and kicks 10 to 15 back dolphin kicks with the arms stretched tightly against the side of the head behind the ears (torpedo). The swimmer surfaces and continues back dolphin kick in the torpedo position through the first 25. The swimmer pushes off in a front position and kicks six to eight dolphin kicks in a submerged torpedo position. The swimmer surfaces with a no-breath butterfly stroke and continues the butterfly stroke, breathing every two strokes, through the second 25.

SUMMARY

1. The dolphin or butterfly kick is used throughout the butterfly stroke and on the starts and turns in crawl and backstroke.
2. For most swimmers, the dolphin kick is faster off the walls than swimming or using a flutter kick.
3. The streamlined torpedo position is essential.
4. The dolphin kick power comes from the hips back through the feet.
5. The dolphin kick must be fast and explosive.
6. Underwater dolphin kicking drills should include fins and monofins.
7. The dolphin kick should be a continuous action.

Chapter 7

CRAWL STROKE

Elements pertinent to all four strokes were discussed thoroughly in chapter 5. Counting the strokes taken to reach a given point, such as one pool length, is a good indicator of the distance covered by each arm stroke. Marking the hand entry and the hand exit points by spotting cones on the pool deck will help swimmers become aware of their distance per stroke. Moving the body past the arm is the desired result of each arm stroke. The hand should exit slightly in front of the point of the hand entry, and spotting cones on the deck will indicate if this is being done.

The two most common kicking patterns in the crawl are the six-beat and the two-beat kicks per arm cycle. Some people are more comfortable using a broken tempo kick that isn't a six- or a two-beat kick. Kicking drills will be the same regardless of the number of kicks used in each complete arm cycle.

Regardless of the kicking rhythm, the hips, body, and legs must rotate throughout the stroke. Body rotation provides additional power and facilitates streamlining, and this rotation must originate from the hips.

STROKE MECHANICS

There are two major considerations in the area of mechanics: One is the actual technique that is best for each individual swimmer, and the second is the best sequence for teaching the skills necessary for a good crawl stroke.

Technical Aspects

When teaching the crawl stroke, focus your instruction on these main areas: Body position, the arm stroke, body rotation, streamlining, the kick, and correct breathing.

Body Position

The buoyancy of each swimmer will be a determining factor in body position on the water. Each swimmer must seek the best body position possible. This is primarily determined by the swimmer's ability to bring the lower body, the hips and legs, close to the water surface. This position offers less resistance to the water when swimming. The head is the key to this control, and moving the eye position to a more downward look will help to lift the lower body parts nearer the surface.

Test your swimmers in a neutral head position while floating. Their eyes should be looking directly downward to the bottom of the pool in a neutral position (90 degrees). Adjust that position to a more forward look from the eyes, and watch the change of depth at the lower body parts. The swimmer can also change basic body position by pressing downward on the chest while floating. Most swimmers carry their heads too high, and their eye position is too far forward. A more neutral head position is advisable for most swimmers.

Arm Stroke

Most of the material that I have read emphasizes sweeps. Sweeps used to be referred to as an S and reverse S pattern, depending on which stroking arm was in use, and more recently as sweeps, usually the out and in sweeps. I'm now convinced that describing the crawl arm stroke as sweeps is outdated. It is the wrong concept to consider.

Some world-class swimmers have advocated a straight-line pull and avoided sweeps for many years. I remember conducting a clinic with Robin Leamy, an American record holder in sprint freestyle, in the mid-1980s. He swam with a straight-line pull and taught the stroke to the clinic swimmers. At that time I wasn't convinced it should be the stroking model.

A few years ago, I visited a training session on the Gold Coast in Australia. Grant Hackett and Ian Thorpe were the two most prominent swimmers in the water. Both were moving water through the stroke in a straight line, at least to the eye. There were no sideward sweeps. Because there were age-group swimmers training at the same time, I observed their crawl stroke technique. Underwater, they were using the same basic technique as both Hackett and Thorpe. More recently I watched the underwater highlights of the finalists at the Sydney Olympic Games. These swimmers moved their arms through the underwater stroke in the same manner as I already described.

The swimmers were using a very effective trunk rotation to apply much of the force on the "anchored" arm. These swimmers were entering the water, making a catch, pressing the fingertips downward, and getting the wrist up over the hand and then the elbow up over the wrist. The hand then followed a downward and backward path extremely close to a straight line. Keeping the elbows high under water is the most necessary component for successfully mastering these phases.

Some overlap of the arms should be taught. Some successful swimmers delay their catch on entry to almost catch up one arm to the other. Others get into their catch quickly with only a little overlap. Use drills that teach an overlap of the arms, but let swimmers adjust their stroke individually. Efficiency drills that optimize the distance per stroke will help each swimmer determine what works best for that swimmer.

A high elbow position during the entry phase will help place the arm into the water cleanly with less resistance and will ensure an effective position to start the underwater arm stroke (figure 7.1). Entry into the water should be made through the same hole with the fingertips entering first, then the wrist, the elbow, and the shoulder. The hand should enter the water at a point between the ear and the tip of the shoulder on the side of the stroking arm. The entry should be about a hand length below the surface of the water. The swimmer should push the elbow forward on entry as the hand moves into the catch and

Figure 7.1   This demonstrates the overlapping of the arms in the crawl stroke. The recovery arm should be well into the recovery before starting the stroking cycle on the in-water and forward arm. The hyphenated line through the center of the head and spine indicates correct body alignment.

keep the inside socket of the elbow pointed slightly downward on the water. This position will help keep the elbows up and help optimize the distance per stroke.

The fingertips must begin to point downward as the catch is completed. This results in a high wrist, which is essential. I believe that this is one of the most neglected technique tips in the teaching of the crawl. Using paddles can help to make this point. I prefer using my Han's Paddles for correcting hand position and teaching the downward pointing of the fingertips. Reversing the Han's Paddle places the tapered end forward, and the paddle rests on the fingertips and only a very small section of the hand. Swimming and drills done with that paddle so attached do much to attain this desired technique. Don't permit a drop of the elbow at this point in the stroke. Teaching swimmers to just stretch out more at this point will too often result in a dropped elbow.

The catch position permits swimmers to feel and engage water firmly on the hand. The initial part, the entry and catch, is most important. The swimmer must get it right at the start in order to have an efficient stroke for the remainder of the arm stroke. The palm should be slightly pitched with the little finger just a bit higher than the thumb. The elbows must be kept up during the underwater strokes. There should be no exceptions to this principle, because it is necessary to establish an "anchored" arm position from which the swimmer can

effectively push the body past the arm during the trunk rotation. Keeping some water pressure on the inside elbow socket, a slightly downward position, will maintain the desired elbows-up position in the arm stroke.

The swimmer should push water off the fingertips as the hand position changes on the water at the finish of the stroke. At the finish, the elbow and wrist should lead the hand slightly to permit it to push water off the fingertips and toward the bottom of the feet. The arm accelerates in the back half of the arm stroke.

The recovery of the arm begins at the peak of the trunk rotation. The hips rotate to their peak just in time to get out of the way of the hand that is finishing the stroke. This correct timing of the hip rotation is necessary to get the most out of the trunk rotation. Too many swimmers miss this hip rotation timing and finish their stroke too early or too late. Correct timing also releases the hand with very little effort into the recovery. When a good release is made, this will get the swimmer into the recovery quickly and smoothly, but if the swimmer continues to push water back, he or she will lose the momentum needed for a good recovery.

The elbows must be kept up during the *underwater* strokes. No exceptions!

The elbows-up position in the recovery will keep the elbow higher than the hand. The arm should be relaxed and bent at the elbow with the hand under or slightly outside of the elbow, and the thumb should lead the hand during the recovery. Teach the high elbow recovery in the crawl arm stroke. There is an occasional exception to this rule: If the swimmer has good tempo and power, despite his or her hand being higher than the elbow in the recovery phase, then don't correct it.

Straight Arm Recovery for the Crawl

My model for the crawl stroke discussion is the elbows-up position in the recovery, however, many great swimmers use a straight arm recovery and I totally accept that style for some swimmers. The important item, in either the elbows-up or in the straight arm recovery, is what the swimmer does with the underwater phase of each arm stroke. The principles that have already been listed apply equally to each style of arm recovery. There will usually be less overlapping of the arms in the straight arm recovery.

There is no one way to swim fast. The style of the arm recovery is a prime example. The important principles of body alignment, the timing of the hip rotation, and the elbows-up anchoring of the arm *under* the water are examples of basic principles that must be followed for fast swimming. The style of arm recovery isn't one of the basic principles. If you have a straight arm recovery swimmer on one or both arms, look at the body alignment, timing, and what occurs under water before making any recovery technique changes. Too many recent world records have been set by straight arm recovery swimmers.

Body Rotation and Streamlining

When I was a young competitive swimmer, I was taught to swim as flat on the water as possible. However, after I started coaching, it became obvious to me that this was not the most efficient way to swim. When the swimmer rotates the body and swims more on the side, the swimmer's body is streamlined, positioned so it creates less resistance and moves faster through the water. Trunk rotation should always be initiated in the hips: The swimmer should think hips, trunk, shoulders, and chin, in that order. Rotating from the hips first facilitates full rotation of the trunk.

Using "pressure points" when swimming crawl or crawl drills will facilitate adequate trunk rotation (see figure 7.2). If the swimmer places the hand under the armpit, the width of that hand plus a point just forward of the center line of that side of the body is the swimmer's pressure point. The swimmer should attempt to press the pressure point down on the water on the entry and catch with both arms. This technique tip also brings the lower parts of the body higher in the water, which decreases resistance.

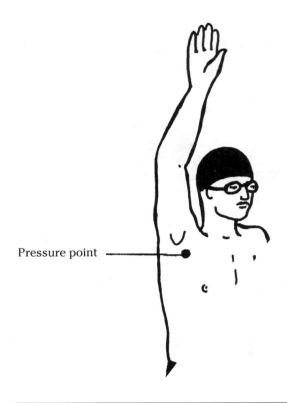

Pressure point

Figure 7.2   Example of a crawl stroke pressure point.

Rotation and Speed

One of the most memorable demonstrations I have ever witnessed occurred at a clinic about 30 years ago, when Coach Howard Firby stretched out a long piece of surgical tubing that was anchored at one corner of the pool and gave it to a swimmer at the other end. The swimmer, holding onto the end of the tubing, was pulled to the other end of the pool.

Coach Firby performed this demonstration twice. The first time the swimmer held the tubing with both hands extended overhead. The swimmer was timed and observed moving in a near-flat position. In the second demonstration, the swimmer held the end of the tubing with only one hand, and as a result naturally turned onto one side. In this position, the swimmer moved considerably faster across the pool and created a much smaller wave in front.

"Tow your buddy," a game described in chapter 12, illustrates the principle behind body rotation and streamlining. When the towed swimmer holds onto the other's leg with both hands, he or she stays flat and creates more water resistance. On the other hand, when the swimmer holds onto the leg with one hand, he or she rolls to the side and lessens the water resistance. I've never had any swimmers who have won a tow your buddy race by holding onto the lead swimmer's leg with two hands.

Teach body rotation and streamlining by having your crawl swimmers picture themselves as though they were skewered on a broom handle. The broom handle is screwed through the top of their head down to their hips. The body rotates on that broom handle from side to side, continuously through each arm cycle, without ever breaking or bending that handle. Swimmers must concentrate on initiating the trunk rotation at the hips. The goal is to keep the body in one straight line throughout the skewered swimmer's side-to-side movement.

The Kick

The kick in the crawl stroke is not just up and down but is also sideward because it follows a rotating body. The body rotation must be in a straight line, and the legs and feet must also kick within this same line, remaining within the boundaries of the eddies created by the upper half of the body. The depth and width of the kick have limits. Teach a streamlined, continuous kick from the hips with flexible knees and ankles.

1. Use drills like the lateral streamlined kicking with one arm extended and one arm back at the side.

2. Have swimmers kick with both arms crossed out in front of the head, rotating from the hips. The crossed arms aid the rotation.

3. Have swimmers kick with both arms back at their sides and rotating the body through the kick.

4. Have swimmers kick with both arms out front and rotating the body through the kick.

These techniques can be done effectively for short distances underwater as well. You can also use fins with any of the kicking drills.

Proper Breathing

Correct breathing skills must be included in learning crawl. Instructing swimmers to breathe every one, two, and three strokes is necessary in teaching crawl breathing, but not in that order. Breathing every two strokes on one favorite breathing side is natural and probably the most used method. However, swimmers need to practice breathing every three strokes in many of their technique drills, because this forces them to breathe on both sides with a balanced stroke.

Balanced body rotation comes by breathing every three strokes. Breathing on only one side can only result in an uneven body rotation. Breathing every stroke is a drill used less often, but I like it to develop faster body rotation. When swimmers breathe every stroke, they develop more hip rotation, or what's known as a hip "pop," which increases their hand speed in the stroke's power phase and speeds them into the recovery.

Breathing while skewered and rotating on a broom handle must result in straight-line swimming. Teach your swimmers to breathe in the trough created by the head as it turns to the side to breathe. As the swimmer's chin follows the shoulder in the body rotation, the head is turned on its side with the ear in the water; the swimmer's eyes should focus on the water surface just a few inches ahead of the mouth as it opens to breathe. The eye position during breathing can also be described as looking at 10 or 2 o'clock, according to which side is used for breathing. This breathing position will keep the majority of your swimmers in a straight line on the skewer during all phases of their body rotation.

Teach your swimmers to breathe without holding their breath. They should exhale slowly at first and time their exhalation so that they can finish with a burst of air as their mouth clears the water surface.

CRAWL STROKE

See the drawing below and note the hand, wrist, elbow, and shoulder entry of the arm. It must be in that order with the wrist above the hand, the elbow above the wrist, and the shoulder above the elbow. This drawing also illustrates the following basic principles in the start of the crawl stroking cycle:

1. The body must be aligned. Imagine a steel rod inserted from the center of the head through the length of the spine as the alignment goal.

2. Lengthen the line by extending the arm forward on entry. Stay long and streamlined to create the least resistance to the water.

3. The hips and trunk are rotated from one side to the other side through a complete stroking cycle. The hips initiate this trunk rotation and the body slides through the water from side to side.

4. The head remains in a neutral position and the breath is taken by rotating the body and not by turning the head.

The following illustrations show the progressive positions of the stroking arm as the hips and trunk rotate.

Position 1

The fingertips begin to point down in a direct line, and the elbow remains above the wrist and fingers.

Position 2

The fingertips point directly down. The elbow is cocked and anchored on the water.

Position 3

The fingertips are pointed down with the wrist in line with the hand at mid-pull. The elbow is up and anchored on the water with the trunk being rotated to drive the body past the anchored arm.

Position 4

The wrist flexes to permit the hand and fingers to continue pushing water back.

Position 5

The exit and beginning of the arm recovery features the elbow leading the recovery at the completion of the armstroke.

The trunk rotation peaks on the start of the arm recovery. Breathing should occur at this point to maintain body alignment. The solid line indicates correct body alignment.

Sequence of Teaching Crawl

Teach a basic arm stroking skill first to give your swimmers some confidence in their ability to move through the water effectively. In those first drills, establish a basic arm stroke technique. In waist-deep water, use a walking drill emphasizing the fingertips, hand, wrist, elbow, and then shoulder entry. This drill is excellent when using Han's Paddles attached in the reverse position (the tapered end forward).

The torpedo streamlined position must be taught as one of the first drills, followed by the kicking and breathing skills. Next, teach the arm stroking drills of maximizing and then optimizing the distance per stroke. With each of these skills effectively in place, you can begin timed speed drills.

SPECIAL TIPS FOR TEACHING THE CRAWL STROKE

Drills are the most effective method of teaching stroke skills, so make sure your swimmers do drills correctly. Drills are 100 percent correct or they are wrong. Monitor the drills carefully, and don't compromise on technique. You can isolate stroking technique points through drills and combine these points into progressions into the complete stroke.

Be a teacher when using stroke drills. Drills need to be explained, demonstrated, and practiced until your swimmers perform them correctly—this is the key to effective learning. Correct drills that use the best technique make perfect practice possible. Don't tolerate drills being done incorrectly. Be exact and expect the best from your swimmers.

Feel of the Water

Teach your swimmers to use their fists only in some drills or while swimming crawl. Then, they should gradually open the hand to better feel the water. Closing the fists removes the sensation of water on the hand; however, when your swimmers reopen their hands, they will have a better perception of the hand on water as a result of the previous absence of sensation. Additional methods of creating water awareness include having your athletes swim with their fingers making the "A-OK" sign or swimming only with the index or "pinky" finger extended to attain better feel of the water.

Similarly, use hand paddles in the same way to attain a better feel. For the best results, you should use different sizes of holed paddles, Han's Paddles, Groovers, and Grippers (see chapter 12).

Fins

Use fins in at least some of your kicking and swimming drills to increase your swimmers' speed and confidence in both areas. Fins also help to streamline the legs while kicking. Try all sizes and shapes of fins to determine what's best for your swimmers. I prefer a soft-shoe type of fin that is comfortable on my swimmers' feet. For the best results, I cut a few inches off the end of these flippers to allow the swimmer to kick at swimming speed. With these shorter fins, your swimmers can kick faster and in the correct range.

Distance and Endurance Considerations

Your teaching of the basic crawl should be the same for all of your swimmers; only when they specialize in a particular sprint or distance event will there be some differences that you need to recognize.

Swimmers at 200 meters and longer distances in crawl will need to breathe every stroke cycle in most instances. Swimmers with a two-beat or broken tempo kick are stroking faster and can breathe every three strokes or one and a half cycles. In these longer events, sustained speed is the goal, and regular breathing makes this a better possibility; teach these swimmers to breathe every cycle or as I have indicated here.

DRILLS FOR THE CRAWL

Next I outline a number of drills that I believe are necessary in teaching new skills or in perfecting learned ones. Some of these drills I rarely use or use only with certain swimmers who may need that special drill. Once your swimmers learn these drills, they can keep coming back to basics by incorporating the drills into their practice sessions and their warm-up at competition. I list the major drills in a sequence that I highly recommend for teaching crawl swimming, but they do not have to be introduced in this exact order.

Hand, Wrist, Elbow

Use a standing drill first in this series. Emphasize, in order, fingertips, hand, wrist, elbow, and shoulders. Have your swimmers stand in waist-deep water and simulate the crawl arm stroke. Isolate or freeze the entry point, hand pitch, high elbow arm recovery, or whatever part you want to be visualized. This drill is very effective when the swimmer can watch his or her stroking while in the water and facing a full-length mirror. The mirror can be at the wall of the shallow end of the pool.

Direct the entry as follows:

1. Fingertips and hand first
2. Then wrist
3. Then elbow
4. Then shoulder

Talk to your swimmers. Call out "hand," "wrist," and "elbow" as the arm goes through this sequence on entry. Have your swimmers also call out this sequence as they go through the hand, wrist, elbow, and shoulder entry. Once you've taught your swimmers the standing drill, have them begin walking through this same drill in waist-deep water. Emphasize that they walk past the hand on each stroke so that they can feel the distance covered in each arm stroke. As they walk, the swimmers will be able to see the point of hand entry and see their bodies going past that point at the hand exit position.

Move from the walking drill to swimming short distances with emphasis on the hand, wrist, and elbow drill. Have your swimmers mentally repeat these words—hand, wrist, elbow—while swimming, just as they verbally called them out in the standing and walking drills. I like to have swimmers move from a couple of strokes standing, to walking a few strokes, and then to swimming the drill for a short distance.

Torpedo

Torpedo is the streamlined position with both arms extended overhead. One hand is on top of the other hand with the thumb of the top hand gripped around the little finger side of the lower hand. Elbows are pulled in tight and the arms are extended. The stomach and buttocks are pulled in tight, and the legs are together and extended fully all the way through the toes. The upper arms are squeezed in just behind the swimmer's ears. This presents a nearly straight line all the way from the top of the swimmer's hands to his or her feet.

Have your swimmers lie on their backs on the pool deck and practice the torpedo position before going into the water. You can adjust some of their faults easily on the deck, emphasizing necessary points by applying some manual pressure where necessary. Have the swimmers practice in the water from the push off the wall position just under the water and its surface tension.

Add a flutter kick to the drill when your swimmers have learned to hold a perfect torpedo position. Teach this for short distances underwater that are comfortable and safe for your swimmers.

Streamlined Lateral Kicking

This kicking drill is done in a lateral position. The swimmer assumes the maximum rotation position of the crawl stroke by extending one arm forward and keeping the other arm at the opposite side of the body. Teach this lateral stretch position precisely, with the extended arm on the lower side of the body and in a spear position as straight as possible with the little finger and the elbow tipped up slightly. The other arm on the higher side is extended back alongside the leg.

Holding the spear position, with the little finger and elbow tipped up, is critical for this lateral drill to be effective. Keeping the inside elbow socket pointed slightly downward ensures that the drill is done right. Do not permit a dropped elbow at any time. Have swimmers practice this drill first on one side and then the other for a given distance, either one length or cross-pool. Try this drill with a "naked" paddle on the hand of the extended arm to help keep the elbow tipped up.

Once this streamlined position has been learned correctly, you can teach swimmers to do 12/12, 8/8, and 6/6 combination drills. In the 12/12 kicking drill, the swimmer kicks 12 times on one side and then rotates and does another 12 kicks on the other side. Holding the speared arm position correctly throughout the 12 kicks and through the rotation on the other side is critical. A 10/10 would include 10-beat kick, a rotation, then 10 more; an 8/8 and 6/6 would include the listed number of kicks, a rotation, and the remaining kicks.

I like combining this kicking drill so that my swimmers start with a 12/12 and then go into a 10/10, then an 8/8, and finally a 6/6. Each repeat of this drill would start and finish the same way. One example might be 10×75 yards: Wherever our swimmers are in their kick count cycle, when they get to 6/6, they hold that kick until that 75 yards is completed, and then they start anew in the next 75 yards.

Shark Fin

This is a variation of the one-arm extended streamline kicking drills. The swimmer recovers the elbow to mid-recovery and holds that elbow in a fixed position with the trunk rotated. The bent arm is the shark's fin. The swimmer should practice this drill on the other side of the body as well.

Breathing Drills

Breathing drills can start at any time and can be combined with some of the drills that I have already listed. Bobbing drills, which teach rhythmic breathing, should be started early for any new swimmer. These can be done in four or five feet of water while the swimmer is standing on the bottom of the pool or even in deep water while holding onto the side of the pool or staying away from the wall. Use bobbing to teach your swimmers the timing of inhaling and exhaling.

You can add breathing to the hand, wrist, elbow drill once it is learned. The standing drill helps swimmers learn to time their breathing to their arm stroke and to develop the correct in-line position of the head when breathing. Breathing is next added to the hand, wrist, elbow walking drills and then to the swimming drills.

You can emphasize the proper head position in breathing with the streamlined kicking drills, and then you can add the breathing timing in the one-arm swim drills.

One-Arm Swims With One Arm Extended

This drill follows the streamlined lateral kicking drills. Emphasize the forward extended position of the speared arm. Your swimmers must keep their little finger and elbow tipped up at all times in this drill. Have your swimmers do the crawl stroke with only the arm that had been at their side during the streamlined lateral kicking drill. They should continue to extend and spear their forward arm as they swim the crawl with one arm.

This is a great drill for streamlining and maximum distance per stroke. Changing the stroking arm every length or every specified number of strokes helps to develop an even stroke throughout the body rotation cycle and facilitates the swimmer's ability to breathe on both sides. Breathing takes place on the side of the stroking arm.

Stretch-Up Swims

Because of the similarity between the drills, stretch-up swims should follow one-arm swims with the arm extended forward. The two drills are similar, except that for stretch-up swims, the swimmer switches to the other arm after each stroke. Both drills stress the main technique points. Stretch-up swims refer to the swimmer stretching one arm up to the other before stroking with that other arm. It is a complete overlapping stroke. Emphasize pushing the elbow forward on entry to control its position better. Although stretch-up swims are good for maximum distance per stroke, they can lead to a dropped elbow position in your swimmers, so monitor them carefully.

One-Arm Swims With the Nonstroking Arm at the Side

When you teach one-arm swimming with the nonstroking arm at the side, teach your swimmers to breathe on the opposite side of their stroking arm and to time their head turn for breathing to the entry of the stroking arm. This drill also requires swimmers to focus more on maintaining the skewered and streamlined swimming position. Once your swimmers learn the drill, have them alternate their breathing side, which will help balance their body rotation.

Hand in Pocket

This is a variation of the one-arm extended drill. The arm at the side of the leg moves in and out of an imaginary pocket. The swimmer initiates the elbow up into the recovery but only recovers one-third of the full recovery. Then the swimmer puts the hand back in the pocket and pushes on the upper thigh to emphasize the full hip rotation at the completion of the underwater arm stroke. The swimmer is emphasizing the peak of the hip rotation at the completion of the underwater arm stroke by pushing lightly on the thigh.

Thumb Drag

Use the thumb drag to teach a high elbow on the arm recovery. Your swimmers recover their arm by dragging the thumb along the body through the armpit. Variations of this drill would be to have your swimmers' "fingers do the walking" on the water through their recovery. A similar drill is the "zipper" recovery, whereby swimmers zipper the hand to the body during the recovery.

Swim the Rope

Stretch a rope the length of your pool and anchor it at both ends, preferably a few inches underwater. Have your swimmers swim the rope by straddling it, gripping it with each hand, and pulling themselves past the gripping hand. This activity teaches maximum distance per stroke and gives your swimmers the feeling of moving the body with the arm. Count the number of strokes your athletes need to swim each length on the rope. Have them return to the other end without swimming on the rope and again count their strokes. They should attempt to maintain the same number of strokes.

Coach George Block, Alamo Area Aquatics, adds a special method for this drill. He uses a 25-yard soft garden hose attached to each end of the pool in place of a rope. The soft garden hose permits learners to avoid dropping their elbows during the pull. I can see the value of this adjustment, and I endorse his "swim the hose" method.

Side Glide Delay

This is another drill by Coach George Block that has a lot of merit. Have the swimmer start in a side glide position, one arm forward and one arm back at the side. The swimmer should watch the palm of the recovering hand until it stops directly over the elbow of the extended arm. The recovering arm should be "frozen" in front of the shoulder and over the water surface. The swimmer returns the head to the centerline to watch the lead hand catch and

cock (this is the anchored elbow-up position of the arm). Then the swimmer snaps both arms to the opposite side glide position.

Transition Drills

Combining drills to follow a logical progression can be an effective way to teach any stroke. Have your swimmers focus on one drill, then move them to others, until they are doing the complete stroke. The transition from drills to regular swimming will carry their good technique forward.

For example, have your swimmers start with a lateral streamlined kick, then progress to one-arm swims with one arm extended, then to stretch-up swims, and finally to swimming the crawl.

Have swimmers try the following kick/swim combination: 9 lateral streamlined kicks, 9 complete swimming strokes, then 7 and 7, then 5 and 5, then 3 and 3.

Another possible progression of drills might include a dog paddle with the head up, a crawl arm pull with underwater recovery and the head up or down, a tip of the elbow out of the water with head up or down, a half arm lift with head down, a wrist drag, a fingertip drag, and then finally swimming crawl. I list these examples only to give you an idea of the countless combinations that you can use to organize your drills into a logical progression.

Optimum Distance Per Stroke Drills

Refer to the chapter 5 description of these drills.

SUMMARY OF CRAWL STROKE

The following hints will help you to teach and coach great crawl:

1. You can permit a variety of kicking rhythms to each arm stroke, but teach a continuous kick.
2. Optimize distance per stroke first; speed can come later.

3. Emphasize high elbows, but adjust accordingly for straight arm recovery swimmers.

4. Stress to your swimmers that their entry is fingertips, then hand, then wrist, then elbow, then shoulder.

5. Have your swimmers push their elbows forward on entry, pointing the elbow socket slightly downward.

6. Teach swimmers to keep fingers pointed downward into the catch position.

7. Teach your swimmers to rotate their bodies as if they were on a skewer.

8. Remember that the depth and width of your swimmers' kicks have limits.

9. Have your swimmers focus their eyes on the water surface just in front of their mouth when breathing, the 10 or 2 o'clock positions.

10. Teach the torpedo position and then the kick.

11. Use drills to teach correct technique.

12. Demand perfection in your drill practice, 100 percent correct.

13. Teach regular breathing patterns as required for each event.

CRAWL STROKE STARTS, TURNS, AND FINISHES

Once you've taught and had your swimmers practice their starts, turns, and finishes, you must incorporate those drills into practice sessions that permit all three skills to be improved through perfect practice. Mental training is also necessary. Have swimmers visualize doing perfect starts, turns, and race finishes. Develop relaxation drills, such as controlled deep breathing or lying down and listening to some easy music, to put your swimmers into a state conducive to mental visualization.

Front Starts

Encourage swimmers to maintain good circulation prior to their start, especially in their hands and feet. The use of dry footwear, gloves, and warm-ups will help them avoid becoming cold and losing the feel for the water. Have them use a dry towel to wipe the starting block and their feet and hands. While swimmers are seated or waiting, have them avoid crossing their legs or arms. Such reminders to your swimmers will promote adequate circulation. Teach them to relax before the starting signal, and they will have a quick reaction.

When teaching your swimmers the "take your mark" position, tell them to concentrate on staying on the balls of their feet and not letting their heels touch the block. They should focus on exploding off the blocks at the starting signal.

Teach the following for your swimmers' stance on the blocks:

1. Toes slightly in
2. Heels slightly out
3. Knees slightly bent
4. Head down or looking down the pool
5. Upper body as high as possible
6. Elbows straight or nearly so
7. Fingers and thumb inside or outside of the feet and gripping the forward edge of the block
8. Total concentration on the starting signal

At the starting signal, the head leads, the hands follow, and the body finishes the action. Emphasize each of the following:

1. Flex the arms first and pull toward the water.
2. Get out, not up, straight from the blocks. Thrust the arms to a 90-degree angle with the head just above the shoulders. Get out as far as possible.

FRONT STARTS

Position 1

In the starting position on the blocks, grab the blocks by bending down and forward from the hips. The knees will be bent slightly and the swimmer's weight is on the balls of the feet. The head looks down and the focus is on the impending starting signal.

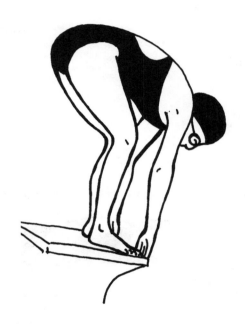

Position 2

React to the starting signal by pushing away with the hands and raising the head quickly. Push from the hands and begin to throw them forward.

Position 3

Driving up and out through the legs, the hands are overlapping for the streamlined entry. The arms and head are still slightly up but in a freeze position.

Position 4

Reach the peak of the start and lower the arms and eyes to prepare for entry.

Position 5

Lower the head inside the arms to begin the streamlining of the body on entry.

3. Drive through the legs, and drive off the blocks with the entire body.

4. Toes should point directly back toward the blocks at the finish of the leg drive.

5. Drop the head between the shoulders and the upper arms just before water entry.

6. Hyperextend to a full torpedo position on entry.

7. Use a hand-on-hand entry through a small hole, kicking out or whipping out, to get the legs through that hole.

8. Point the toes on entry and glide only long enough to take full advantage of the dive momentum.

Many swimmers prefer the track start. Swimmers begin with both feet forward, step back with one leg, and keep the heel up on the back leg. The back leg should be positioned well back on the blocks. Swimmers should grip tight, lean back, drive off the back leg first, and then throw themselves into a normal starting position off the front leg at the starting signal. Relay starts should use a form of rolling start. Swimmers shouldn't use grab starts on relays.

Teaching tips for the crawl start include the following:

1. Swimmers should hold the velocity as long as possible by kicking hard and using shallow and very quick dolphin kicks (see chapter 6) as soon as they enter the water. They should switch to flutter kick on the breakout strokes.

2. The swimmer should accelerate the first arm pull all the way through the finish. The swimmer's head should still be under the surface water tension until near the finish of the first arm stroke.

3. The swimmer should finish the pull, lift the head, and break out or "surf" through the surface.

4. Swimmers should ride the water high as they go into the first surface arm stroke. Have them stretch the nonpulling arm out front during the first surface stroke to streamline as much as possible.

Special drills for improving the racing start include starting off the 1-meter diving board and starting from the starting blocks using one hand paddle on the hand of the arm taking the first arm stroke. Swimmers should always practice starts in deep water to avoid injury.

Turns

The key to great turns is to teach, expect, and demand them in practice. Emphasize the following steps in teaching the crawl turn:

1. Swimmers must build speed on the approach to every wall, because the momentum they have going into the wall will determine how fast they get off from the wall; the faster they can come into a wall, the faster they will come off it.

2. Swimmers need to get the nose to the knees and the heels to the hips on the turn. Teach a compact tuck position for your swimmers' turns.

3. Swimmers should pull out with the lower arm first and shouldn't breathe on this first arm stroke.

4. Swimmers must kick off the wall with very fast, shallow dolphin kicks before switching to the flutter kick for the breakout strokes.

5. Swimmers should streamline into the full torpedo position off each wall underwater and under the surface tension.

Following are some special drills to improve turns:

1. No-wall turning drills—fast turns at specific points in the pool, or after so many strokes, but all without a turning wall

TURNS

Position 1

Raise the head slightly to initiate a stronger, faster tuck and dolphin kick into the turn. Always build your speed approaching the wall to gain speed into and out of the turn. The finish of the last arm stroke leads directly into the tight tuck and turn.

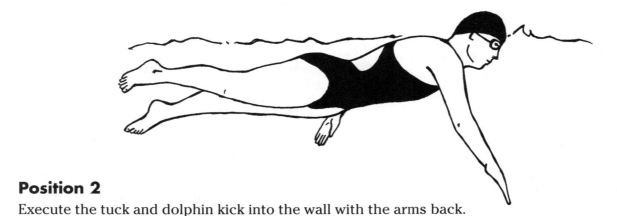

Position 2

Execute the tuck and dolphin kick into the wall with the arms back.

Position 3

The feet are on the wall and in line with the body for the push off the wall.

Position 4

The balls of the feet are pushing off the wall and the body is on the back and side.

Position 5

Take a streamlined torpedo position off the wall.

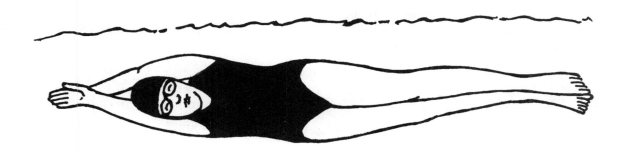

2. Submerged turns—the swimmer dives under the water at the backstroke flags and kicks into a fast submerged turn
3. Turning drills using one and two pairs of hand paddles—both on the wall and without a wall

Finishes

Your swimmers should finish with an arm fully stretched and their body rolled to one side; this position will give them added inches to the length of their arm at the finish. Your swimmers must keep their ear on their shoulder at the finish so that their head remains in the water through the completion of the wall touch. Emphasize that they keep the flutter kick going—so as to drive themselves into the wall—until they touch the wall.

The value of an efficient race finish can't be overemphasized. I'm especially proud of my swimmers when they win the close ones. Close races are won by the swimmers who have practiced great finishes. Frequently in my practice sessions, I include a few minutes at the end of a workout for finish drills.

Winning Close Races

Several years ago, I started doing finish drills on a regular basis throughout the season. The first season we won two very close races because of that special training emphasis on finishes. In a major meet in Las Vegas, one of our high school girls won an 800-yard free relay for our Tacoma Swim Club against some good college swimmers. Also, one of our high school boys at the high school state championship meet in the 100-yard free out-touched a rival who was ahead as they moved to the finish wall.

SUMMARY FOR CRAWL STROKE STARTS, TURNS, AND FINISHES

1. Prepare your swimmers both mentally and physically for front starts.
2. Your athletes must start by going out and not up.
3. Teach your swimmers to dive through one hole.
4. Expect and demand great turns in practice.
5. Teach your swimmers the correct race finish position.

Chapter
8
BACKSTROKE

Backstroke and crawl are long-axis strokes. Much of what is true for the crawl applies also to backstroke. Stroke length, stroke frequency, and stroke count apply to all four competitive strokes. Trunk rotation, a flutter kick, and alternating arm strokes apply only to backstroke and crawl.

Success in backstroke and crawl technique is best achieved with rhythm, relaxation, and rotation. Rhythm facilitates power, the result of trunk rotation. Rotation refers to the hip-initiated trunk rotation that generates stroking power and reduces drag. Relaxation helps the swimmer maintain sustained stroking power. The arm recovery and breathing pattern are two main components of relaxation.

Rhythm requires the body to move past the anchored arm, the arm underwater, evenly and with constant propulsion.

The timing of the trunk rotation to arm recovery and entry is a major key to effective rhythm. The ideal technique is to rotate the hips out of the way of the arm and hand that are finishing the stroke. This puts the hips to the highest point on their side as the hand is finishing the stroke.

Correct timing permits the arm and hand to finish the stroke and to get into the recovery cleanly. The torque action also unloads the weight of the hips and reduces drag. This will result in good shoulder rotation and a stroking level depth for the catch on the hand entry. The trunk rotation follows the most effective rhythm timing and, done properly, will facilitate a thumb-first exit, vertical recovery, and a little-finger catch on entry, all of which are essential components for successful backstroke.

Relaxation essentially requires the arms to recover naturally in a ballistic type of recovery, as opposed to lifting or carrying the arms into the recovery. The arm and hand also "fall" into the entry, as opposed to being carried and placed into the entry. A regular breathing pattern, inhaling on one arm and exhaling on the second arm, also is important for relaxation.

BACKSTROKE

Position 1

Make the arm entry to the little finger side of the hand. The catch is made underwater at stroking level depth. The catch must be deep enough to secure an anchored arm position, but not so deep as to necessitate up and down sweeps of the arm.

1. The body must be aligned. As in the crawl stroke, a steel rod through the center of the head down through the spine should be a straight line. This is indicated by the straight line drawn.
2. The hips and trunk are rotated from one side to the other side through a complete stroking cycle.
3. The head is stable and rests aligned in a neutral position in the water.

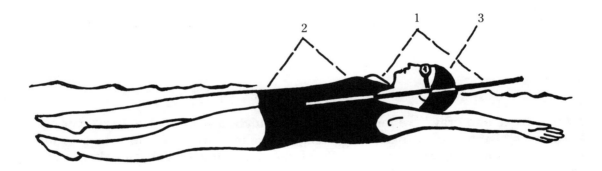

Position 2

The stroking arm is cocked and beginning to bend as it approaches the shoulder line.

Position 3

The stroking arm attains its maximum arm bend as the body is pushed past the anchored arm.

Position 4

The wrist flexes to permit the hand to continue pushing back as the stroking arm nears the completion of that stroke.

Position 5

The hips and trunk have rotated to the other side as the thumb-first arm recovery begins.

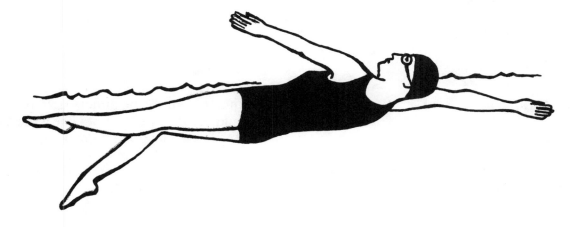

OPTIMIZE THE DISTANCE PER STROKE

The optimum stroke length is the number of strokes per pool length that is most effective for each individual; this is explained in chapter 5. Maximizing the distance per stroke, in itself, isn't the desired end. Rather, optimizing the stroke length to achieve the most effective reference for sustained speed and to achieve the optimum effective stroking rate is the desired goal in all the competitive strokes. The kick, the arm stroke, and coordinated swimming make up the components that through drills, practice, and training contribute to backstroke success.

Body Position

The best backstroke swimmers lie well back on the water with their head close to flat on the water. In the neutral position, the eyes look directly upward at 90 degrees. The swimmer can adjust that position so that the eyes, instead of looking directly overhead, are at a position just short of that with the chin tilting slightly toward the throat (figure 8.1). Your swimmers can simulate this body position by lying their heads back on a very soft pillow.

In the pool, then, you can adjust the swimmer's head accordingly to bring the body and legs up higher in the water. You can also use a pressure point midway on the back between the shoulders. Applying downward pressure at this point will also bring the body and legs higher. The swimmer's chest is out of the water, and the hips should be up high in the water. This position decreases water resistance during swimming.

Kicking

The kick is a very important component of successful backstroke. Legs are important in every push-off from the wall in starts and turns when the butterfly dolphin kick is used

Figure 8.1 The arm is vertical and straight during recovery in the backstroke. The correct head position is also demonstrated here.

to attain the fastest underwater speed as well as great breakout speed into the surface strokes. This kick was discussed in chapter 6.

Backstroke flutter kick is also very important to backstroke success. It maintains surface speed and good body position, and it keeps drag to a minimum. When using the back flutter kick, the swimmer actually rolls from side to side due to good trunk rotation. The kick is best when it is continuous and operates in a relatively narrow range. This will keep the body position more streamlined throughout the swimming stroke.

Beginners need to learn to relax their feet and allow them to rotate in the kick. "Shaking" a shoe or sock off the foot while sitting in the gutter and practicing the back kick is a good beginning step for beginners. I've used that technique for decades, but I like what Coach Debbie Potts has done by making a game of this. Who can shake a sock off the foot first? Keeping it fun for young swimmers always helps to keep them in the sport.

BACKSTROKE FLUTTER KICK DRILLS

Kicking With Arms at Side

First, have the swimmer start with a flat body position to attain the best body position for backstroke. Help each swimmer adjust the direction in which his or her eyes focus to help get the ribcage and hips up high in the water. Pressing downward on a back pressure point at midshoulders, adjusted slightly lower or higher as necessary, can help the swimmer achieve proper body position on the water.

Count six kicks to each arm cycle of both arms and repeat. This helps to develop a continuous kick and to position a starting point on the rhythm of the kick to the arms (six kicks to each arm cycle).

Arms Extended Overhead in Streamlined, Torpedo Kick on the Back

This is a flat position that is not a true position for backstroke; however, it develops the legs and improves the flexibility of the streamlined position that is so vital in the starts and turns. The best body position for each swimmer will vary. The fingertips should be slightly off the water in this drill to get the ribcage higher and to increase the pressure on the legs slightly. This kicking position should also be repeated cross-pool over 10 to 15 yards without fins.

Cross-Pool Kicking Underwater

In this drill, the arms are extended overhead, and the swimmer uses a back flutter kick. This drill helps swimmer to streamline the kick and keep it in a narrow range. This drill can also be effectively done with short swim fins but not cross-pool. Use the main pool and the normal pool length for fin kicking.

Kicking With Both Arms at Side Using Trunk Rotation

The swimmer kicks a set number of kicks on one side and then rotates the trunk to the other side and kicks the same number of kicks.

Kicking With Both Arms Extended Overhead Using Trunk Rotation

Again, the swimmer kicks a set number of kicks on one side and then rotates the trunk to the other side and kicks the same number of kicks.

Kicking With Both Arms Folded or Crossed Behind Head Using Trunk Rotation

Emphasize rotating from the hips but driving the elbows downward on each side. This will also encourage a deep catch when the arm stroke drills are added.

One Arm Extended and One Arm at Side of Body in Trunk-Rotated Position

Use "pressure points" to assist swimmers with kicking on the side. Focus on a pressure point that is one hand width below the armpit and slightly behind the center point of that side. When the swimmer applies water pressure on the pressure point, the swimmer should get the ribcage higher in the water, get the hips and legs up as well, and attain the desired position to the side. The pressure point can be adjusted up or down to meet the needs of each individual swimmer.

The "side" indicates a near 45-degree rotation. Drill on each side using 12-beat kicks on one side then 12 on the other, followed by 10/10, 8/8, and 6/6 kicks on each side. The swimmer should stabilize the head and use the hips to rotate the trunk from side to side. Short swim fins can be added to this kicking drill. Another variation is to scull with the extended hand with or without a "naked" paddle.

Arm Stroke and Coordination

I believe that the up and down movements (sweeps) of the stroking arm should be minimized. My observations of the underwater strokes of champion backstroke swimmers indicate that the pull is very close to a straight line. This is achieved by rotating the trunk past the "anchored" arm. This is a little more difficult to achieve in backstroke than in crawl. It takes more strength than the crawl; however, that should be the goal. Swimmers must be deep enough on the entry and catch to enable a fairly straight line pull. If the entry is too deep then this in-line pull is difficult to achieve.

Making a stroke-level depth catch and maintaining a straight arm for about the first half of the underwater arm stroke facilitate a more direct or straight-line pull-through. Bending the arm too early in the pull is an error that should be avoided. When the arm bend occurs at about the halfway point, then the trunk rotation in the back half of the stroke can affect maximum power from that arm stroke. This comes from the anchored arm position when the arm is bent or cocked.

Up and down movements (sweeps) of the stroking arm should be minimized.

The arm stroke is most effective when the hand is able to maintain the maximum hand surface and "hold" on the water. Videotaping backstroke swimmers has illustrated to me that too many swimmers pull with the thumb leading the little finger, when the thumb should be pointed upward. This technique results in slicing or slipping the hand through the water when the swimmers should attempt to attain an anchored position on the water with the hand and elbow. The anchored position is to have the elbow pointed downward and the hand perpendicular to the surface. The properly timed trunk rotation then helps drive the body past the arms.

The best arm stroke is one that has the arm entering and exiting at close to the same spot on the water. This doesn't happen when the hand is being "sliced" through the water. Place a full-length mirror on the deck at the end of the backstroke lane. I did so for most of my coaching career. It saves a lot of talking, and the pictures that your backstroke swimmer sees are precise and very accurate feedback. Always have the backstroke flags legally in place at every practice session.

The width of the pull is an individual adjustment. The swimmer must feel water well while stroking. The hip rotation generates power in the arm strokes. U.S. Olympian Lea Mauer said that her arm recovery was initiated by her thinking "hips," not shoulders. This emphasizes that trunk rotation starts with the hips. Good shoulder rotation is essential for backstroke success but it must start from the hips. Lea said that once the right hand has made its catch, then she begins to think about rotating that right hip to the up position. The hip then leads the arm and gets out of the way at the finish and start of the recovery.

The progressions in the arm stroke and full stroke that I believe are essential depend on the swimmer's ability level. Master the basic technique drills before moving on to advanced drills. All swimmers need to review basic drills on occasion.

ARM DRILLS

Double Bent Arm Stroke Finishes

The arms recover underwater to a point no higher than the hips and then push back and down below the heels of the feet simultaneously.

Double Bent Arm Strokes for the Back Half

The arms recover underwater to a point no higher than the shoulders and then push back through the finish simultaneously.

Double Arm Stroking

The arms recover over the water, touching or passing close to each other at the peak of the recovery, and then stroke underwater simultaneously. This helps to attain a vertical recovery and to get the arms entering near the 12 o'clock position.

Single Bent Arm Finishes

This builds on the double bent arm stroke finish, but it uses trunk rotation as well. The arm recovers underwater to a point no higher than the hips and then pushes water through the finish. The hip on that side of the body is rotated upward through that stroke finish. This can be done in any combination. Have the swimmer complete a specified number of left arm and then right arm finishes, for example, two left, three right, and so on.

Single Bent Arm Strokes for the Back Half

This is the same as the double bent arm strokes for the back half except it is done single arm with trunk rotation. It can be done in combinations as in the single bent arm finishes.

One-Arm Swims With Opposite Arm Stationary at Side of Body

Rotating the hip to the side as the arm finishes the stroke helps the timing and rhythm of the trunk rotation. The swimmer's swim suit should be visible and clear of the water at the hip on the rotated upper side on this drill. Variations of this drill can include doing a specific number of strokes on one side before changing sides. One example would be four left arm strokes and then four right arm strokes. This drill facilitates the feel of moving the body past the anchored and stroking arm.

One-Arm Swims With Opposite Arm Carried Vertically and Directly Above Shoulder

Emphasize the shoulder extension as the stroke arm makes the entry and catch. This helps to maintain a steady, strong kick and a stroking level depth catch position.

Touchdown Swims

Touchdown swims are one-arm swims that alternate the arms after every stroke. The stroking arm must finish at the side before the other arm resting at the side is permitted to recover and stroke to that side. Since the arms are at the side, I call this a touchdown to the side before recovering the other arm. This drill emphasizes all of the points of the one-arm swims with one arm at the side and adds to the feel and timing of the hip/trunk rotation.

Touch and Go

The touch and go drill emphasizes hip/trunk rotation and shoulder rotation and emphasizes the vertical "rifle barrel" recovery of the arms and a stroking level depth catch of the hands. This drill also encourages a continuous and strong kick. The swimmer recovers one arm to the highest vertical position, directly over the shoulder/chin area, and then holds that arm in a frozen position until the other arm recovers to that same position. The other arm then assumes the frozen position as the previous frozen arm takes its stroke. The swimmer continues to alternate the arm stroke from the frozen vertical spot. This drill should always progress to using hand paddles.

Backstroke Swims With Plastic Coin Purse Balanced on Forehead

This teaches swimmers to stabilize the head position.

Corkscrew Drills

These help the swimmer attain the feel of the trunk moving past the arm during the stroke. The swimmer swims a set number of strokes in freestyle and then a set number of strokes in backstroke (e.g., 7 and 7, 5 and 5, and 3 and 3). The transition from back to crawl and from crawl to back makes the swimmer aware of the trunk moving past the anchored hand and elbow. The 7 and 7 drill would include seven strokes crawl and then seven strokes of backstroke following the rotation of the body into the new stroke. Hand paddles are strongly recommended in this drill because they facilitate a greater awareness of the trunk moving past the arms, especially on the transition stroke.

Spin-Out Drills

These help the swimmer attain an entry near the 12 o'clock position, a vertical rifle barrel recovery, and a "fall in" arm entry. Have the swimmer sit up high in the water as though in an undersized bathtub and then spin and throw his or her arms into a rapid backstroke turnover.

Swim the Rope

Attach a rope to each end of the pool underwater (four to six inches underwater). Have the swimmer swim on one side of the rope going down the pool and then with the other arm on that same side of the rope coming back. This drill gives the feeling of anchoring the hand and elbow on the water and rotating the trunk past the stationary arm. It also helps to maximize the distance per stroke, and hold closely to a more level armstroke pull.

Fist Drills

I recommend that the swimmer use a closed fist on any of the swimming drills to facilitate recognizing the feel of the water on the hands. The swimmer can gradually open the hand after some fist swimming.

Look at all your swimmers from as many viewpoints as possible. This is especially important for backstroke swimmers because they can constantly see you looking at them. The result is better focus on good technique. Watch the swimmers from a high overhead viewpoint—a diving board, high ladder, or some elevated platform—and underwater. When on the deck, move from end to end and side to side. Howard Firby taught me to look at my swimmers by bending over with my back to them and then peering out at them looking back under my armpit. You will see eddies and water flow like never before.

Hand paddles and short fins should be used in all of the swimming drills. Build from basic drills to more advanced drills and then in combination drills to full stroke, but teach the drills in isolation first. Combinations such as six easy crawl strokes and then six fast backstroke arm cycles will also help to perfect backstroke.

Great technique is the result of perfect practice. Every drill must be taught correctly and then repeated in perfect form. Move from drills to the full coordinated stroke in your training sessions. Persistence is one of the most vital coaching traits. Be persistent, and never compromise on technique. Find many ways to say the same thing if necessary, and always remember that one picture is worth a thousand words.

SUMMARY OF BACKSTROKE TECHNIQUE

The following teaching and coaching hints will make fast backstroke swimming a reality for your swimmers:

1. Teach the backstroke in a similar manner to crawl.
2. Teach a back butterfly kick for use off the wall in the start and turns.
3. Make sure your swimmer's body rotates on a skewer in backstroke, as well as crawl.

4. Use optimum stroke per distance drills once the basic skills are learned.

5. Teach the kick first in backstroke.

6. Use a rifle barrel recovery.

7. Teach a thumb-first exit into the recovery.

8. Teach a little finger entry.

9. Have swimmers make a stroking level depth catch.

10. Teach your swimmers to enter at a position slightly short of 12 o'clock.

11. Emphasize the torpedo position early in backstroke.

12. Teach lateral streamlined kicking as it is actually done in backstroke.

13. Use a wall mirror when teaching backstroke.

14. Use paddles as a natural progression in the drills.

15. Teach drills in isolation and then in combination.

16. Combine back and crawl changeovers to emphasize body rotation.

BACKSTROKE STARTS, TURNS, AND FINISHES

The same principles for teaching and practicing crawl stroke starts, turns, and finishes hold true in the backstroke. Expect perfect practice and tolerate no exceptions, if you want the best in competition.

Back Starts

For the backstroke start, the rules require the swimmer to be on the wall with the toes underwater. The back start should be practiced only in deep water.

The backstroke can be broken down into six categories:

1. **Feet placement.** The feet should be placed on the wall at about armpit width. After the swimmer places the feet, the toes should turn to the inside to help spread them slightly and help them stick to the wall. The hips should be kept away from the heels. The toes

BACK STARTS

Position 1

Note the tight tuck on the wall prior to the starting signal. This is a stable position with the hips away from the feet.

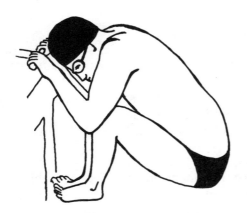

Position 2

The push of the hands away from the starting blocks and the snap of the head back at the starting signal are illustrated. The legs will follow through in this drive from the wall.

Position 3

Throw the arms in a lateral direction and not vertically to get the hips up over the water. The body is arching into the peak of the dive.

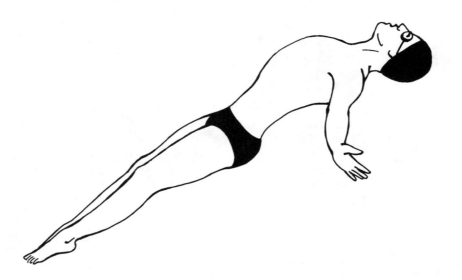

Position 4

Dive through the entry into the water with the upper body. Lift the legs and streamline on entry.

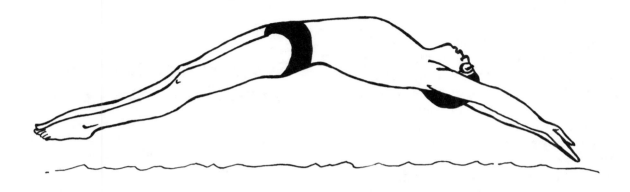

should be kept high, just below the surface and on the same plane. Swimmers should force the toes into the wall and not down the wall.

2. **The grip.** Swimmers should place their thumbs on the upside of the backstroke starting bar.

3. **On the wall and start.** Swimmers must keep the head and back lined up or curl the head into the blocks slightly. The heels are not quite on the wall. On the command, "Take your mark," the swimmer should pull up as high as is comfortable to the level of gravity. The hips are about 80 to 90 degrees away from the heels.

4. **Off the wall.** Swimmers should get some snap from the head and use the upper body in the throw. The hands, head, and shoulders should snap back at once. The arms are just ahead of the legs, and the legs must explode off the wall. Swimmers should lift the core of the body by throwing the arms back in a lateral direction as they leave the wall and then continue the throw of the arms around and

down. This will bring the hips up over the water and will set up the entry.

5. **Entry.** Swimmers should dive through the entry with the upper body. On entry, swimmers must lift the legs and get to the streamlined torpedo position. Take full advantage of the dive's entry speed and then have your swimmers break into the kick with small, fast butterfly kicks to get the most momentum off of the dive. Swimmers should use this kick only to the momentum peak or no further than the 15 meters of underwater kicking that's permitted by the rules. Then swimmers should switch to the flutter kick for the breakout.

6. **Breakout.** Swimmers should start the second arm pull earlier than in normal backstroke swimming on the breakout. The arms overlap in this second arm pull and, as a result, pop swimmers up with more momentum into their regular surface strokes. Swimmers must get up on the breakout, get the hips up, and drive with the flutter kick.

Turns

The backstroke turn is the same as the crawl turn after rolling onto the front according to the rules. Have the swimmers gauge their distance from the wall by using the backstroke flags; they should roll over and execute a forward flip turn on the final approach. Make certain that you always have backstroke flags in place and practice legal turns only. Swimmers can leave their back as they begin the final arm recovery and take one stroke as they somersault into the turn on their front. This turn is to be executed in one continuous motion, and no hand touch is required.

Teach your swimmers to build their speed as they go into the wall. You need to measure their stroke rates in their wall approach to remind them to accelerate at these points in the race. Keep the butterfly kick going through the somersault.

Teach swimmers to perform several fast back butterfly kicks off of each wall before going back into the flutter kick on the breakout strokes. The number of butterfly kicks will depend on the individual swimmer's ability and the rules restricting underwater kicking distances.

Finishes

Teach your backstroke swimmers to finish in a manner similar to the crawl finish, with an arm fully stretched and the body rolled to the side but still legally on the back. Swimmers must keep their heads well back through the wall touch and keep kicking to drive them into the wall.

SUMMARY FOR BACKSTROKE STARTS, TURNS, AND FINISHES

1. Swimmers should throw the arms laterally, then around and down, off the back start.
2. Teach swimmers to use the roll turn.
3. Instruct your swimmers to stretch to the side when touching the wall at the finish.
4. Have swimmers use the dolphin kick off the start and turns in the underwater segments.

Chapter 9

BREASTSTROKE

The first successful crossing of the English Channel was done in breaststroke. It is considered to be the first competitive swimming stroke. The stroke has changed more during my coaching career than any other stroke because the rules that govern it have changed several times. Breaststroke is the least efficient of the four competitive strokes. The swimmer encounters more frontal resistance in it than in any of the others. It is the only stroke in which the arms and legs remain in or almost in the water throughout its entirety. There are many style variations in breaststroke, but the basic principles are the same.

STROKE MECHANICS

In breaststroke, when your swimmers leave each wall, their arms start first. It is unique to the other competitive strokes in this regard. In breaststroke, swimmers pull with their arms first and then kick during the latter part of the arm recovery.

There are two major versions of breaststroke, known as the "flat" and "wave" styles. Mike Barrowman set world records in breaststroke using the wave style, taught by his coach from Hungary, Joseph Nagy. This has become the dominant method of breaststroke. I will cover the essentials of breaststroke swimming, and most are similar for all styles of breaststroke. However, my model is the wave breaststroke.

Your philosophy of teaching breaststroke should be to get the most propulsion possible out of the arms and the legs with the least amount of frontal resistance. You also want to develop a flowing rhythm to the swimmer's stroke. In the wave style, the swimmer

This is the starting and ending position of the breaststroke stroking cycle. It is a streamlined "platform" position with the back of the head and the spine in alignment

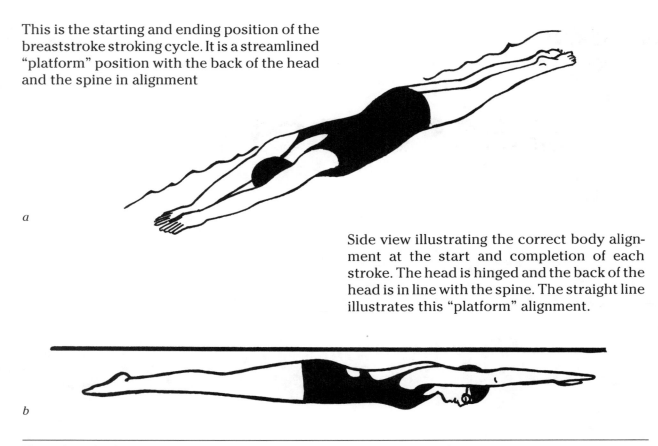

a

Side view illustrating the correct body alignment at the start and completion of each stroke. The head is hinged and the back of the head is in line with the spine. The straight line illustrates this "platform" alignment.

b

Figure 9.1 *(a)* Overview of streamlined position; *(b)* side view of streamlined position.

follows the angle of a wave, and his or her head and shoulders come up out of the water at the completion of the in scull. This allows the upper body to break free of much of the frontal resistance and to lunge forward through the kick, reaching a very streamlined position out front in the stroke (figure 9.1a and b).

> **In the breaststroke, get the most propulsion possible out of the arms and the legs with the least amount of frontal resistance.**

Technical Aspects

The hands scull and pull outward from the extended position out front at the start of the stroke. This outward scull is done with the hands pitched outward, thumbs down, and little fingers pointed upward. This out scull

must reach a point outside of the elbow line. This line will also be outside the shoulders, but the swimmer must avoid pulling too far back. The face remains down in the water during the out scull. The arms remain straight in the out scull and relatively close to the water surface (figure 9.2).

During the rotation from the out scull to the in scull, the elbows are bent and set high with the hands deeper in the water. The elbows must reach a set position before the powerful in scull of the hands can begin. This set or anchored position of the elbows is reached when the elbows are vertically over the forearms and hands. The out scull sets the stage for the power phase of the in scull.

The thumbs take the lead on the in scull and the speed of the pull is accelerated. There should be pressure on the hands and forearm up to the elbow during the in scull. The elbows should maintain an anchored position on the water. The hands should come almost together at the end of the in scull, and the

The hands are pitched with the thumb down. The out pull is made with the face in the water and straight arms. Make an attempt to anchor your hands on the water and pull the body toward the hands.

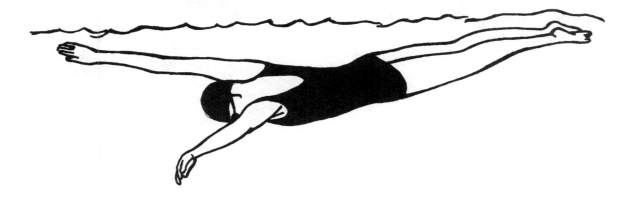

Figure 9.2   Hands out during scull.

elbows should rotate inward to a point inside of the shoulders. This inward hand scull can be directed toward the upper chest. However, it must begin to move forward nearing the end of the in scull so that it finishes nearer the chin level. This will ensure a more efficient lunge and kick forward into the streamlined position out front.

The head begins to come up during the in scull, and the hands and shoulders move forward. Swimmers can arch the back some to slide out and through the water in preparation for the lunge forward on the recovery. Swimmers should attempt to push the pelvis forward after completing the inward sculling. The elbows are under the shoulders in preparation for the lunge. The back of the head is in line with the spine so that it appears to be an extension of the back. The eyes are looking down and forward on the water surface (figure 9.3).

You should be able to see the back of the upper arms out of the water at the peak of the wave. The back of the arms under the armpits should rise to a "dry" position during the in sweep. They should "hunch up" at the shoulders and elbows in preparation to lunge forward through a small hole. The shoulders shrug to the ears, and the elbows are under the shoulders; they should not come together or touch each other.

Have your swimmers blow air out, finishing their exhalation as the head lifts. They should breathe just after they finish the exhalation. At the peak of the lift, their eyes should look forward and down.

The elbows should be high on the water at the end of the in scull and the hands just in front of the chin. The hands should be close to the water surface and in line with the elbows. The hands may be slightly higher than the elbows at the completion of the in scull, but they should attempt to lunge with the elbows in line with the hands and driving the hands forward. The swimmer must get the pelvis and buttocks back up on the lunge forward. The back of the head and the spine should be in line at the end of the recovery or lunge of the arms. The eyes and face are in a downward position at this point. This is the streamlined platform position that is essential at the completion of the breaststroke and butterfly arm strokes.

Teach your swimmers to reenter by lunging forward over the water with the upper body. The head and shoulders should move forward and not down. Have them use their full body on the lunge. The head, back, and hips should be aligned at the finish of the lunge.

As the hands start forward, the heels begin to come up. The knees should be no wider than the hips on the leg recovery. The heels

Use the high elbows as an anchored hinge on the water for the inward scull of the hands and forearms. The head and shoulders rise during the in sweep and breathe on the head rise. Keep the head in the same position while the body rises as a single unit and continue to look slightly forward and downward. The head remains hinged to the trunk with the back of the head close to alignment with the back of the spine.

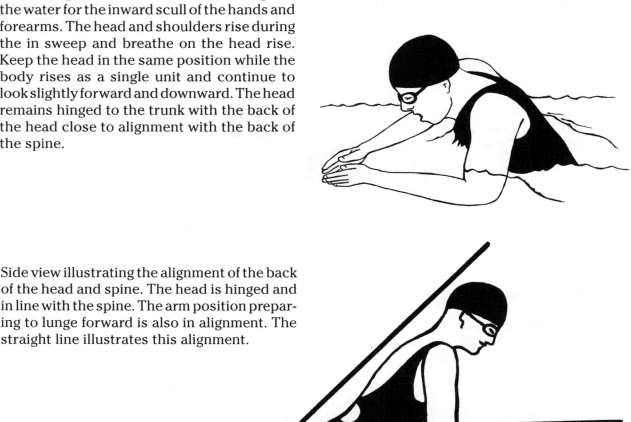

Side view illustrating the alignment of the back of the head and spine. The head is hinged and in line with the spine. The arm position preparing to lunge forward is also in alignment. The straight line illustrates this alignment.

Figure 9.3   Head and spine alignment.

are drawn up quickly without much effort. Your swimmers' knees should be barely under the hip line, and the heels should draw up toward the buttocks. This action reduces the angle at the hip joint, and as a result, frontal resistance is minimal. The heels stay very close as they are drawn up.

At the peak of the heels' recovery, have your swimmers point their toes out before kicking. The heels move outside of the knees rotating down and back. Pressure must be maintained on the soles of the feet through the kick. The kick should accelerate through the completion. The heels finish together with the soles of the feet turned inward toward each other. Teach swimmers to point the toes backward at the finish.

The kick properly timed will fit each swimmer's arm stroke, and vice versa. If the kick is too wide, it can delay the arm stroke. An arm stroke too wide or too long can nullify a great kick. It is up to the coach to use the breaststroke drills, and particularly the optimum distance per stroke drills, to determine the adjustments necessary for each swimmer.

Emphasize the following points in teaching and coaching breaststroke:

1. The swimmer should hold water in the hands, forearms, and feet.

2. The toes hold water in a maximum flexed position as long as possible throughout the kick; follow through from the flexed position at the end of the kick only.

3. The swimmer should keep the eye position somewhat fixed, down and forward, to avoid any major head and eye movement.

4. The swimmer's head drops back into the water in line with the spine as he or she attains the full forward arm extension.

Sequence of Teaching Breaststroke

Sculling drills were covered in chapter 5. These can be expanded into the breaststroke pull. Teach the kick first, and then build the stroke from there. You may need to be a mechanic with some of your swimmers, moving their legs manually to attain the feel of an effective breaststroke kick.

Timing the arms and legs should come next. Use the following sequence: pull by sculling outward and then sculling inward, lunge forward and kick through the end of the lunge.

Teach breathing next and then add it to your timing drills in the following order: pull out, in, breath, lunge, and kick.

SPECIAL TIPS FOR TEACHING THE BREASTSTROKE

Teach and use drills to help your swimmers attain good breaststroke technique, following the same procedures outlined previously in this book. Explain, demonstrate, and then have your swimmers practice until they learn the technique. Expect the best from swimmers in their drill work, and praise them when they do well.

KICKING DRILLS

Face Down on Pool Deck

Manually move the swimmers' legs by drawing the heels up toward the buttocks, turning the toes outward, and pressing the palms of your hands against the soles of their feet. This deck drill focuses on drawing the heels up and not pulling the knees under the body. It also focuses on the catch position of the feet on the water at the top of the leg recovery.

Sitting in the Gutter With Legs Extended Into Water

Swimmers draw the heels down and back until the heels touch the wall. At this point the toes turn outward and circle back and upward through the kick. Don't permit the leg recovery to start at the knees, either spreading or lifting the knees; instead, the kick should start in the heels.

Back Breaststroke Kick

The beginning back breaststroke kick done sitting in the gutter can be extended directly into the water. It can be done first with the arms at the sides of the legs and then with the preferred method of having the arms extended over the head in a streamlined torpedo position. Teach your swimmers to initiate that kick by drawing the heels down and back toward the buttocks. Avoid lifting the knees out of the water or spreading the knees outside of the heels.

Arms Extended Streamlined Kicking

Next, teach swimmers to kick breaststroke in the streamlined torpedo position with both their arms extended out front and with their faces in the water. Have swimmers do this for short distances above and below the surface of the water.

Launching Drill

After teaching the streamlined, arms-extended kicking position, I teach the launching drill to my breaststrokers. The coach must stand in water from waist to shoulder depth with his or her back braced against the pool wall. Your swimmer should face away from you in the front extended arm torpedo position. Place each of the swimmer's feet into each of your hands. Hold the feet so that you are exerting hand pressure on the soles of the feet. Straighten your elbows, and then have the swimmer kick back against your braced arms so he or she is launched forward through the water. From the resistance provided, the swimmer learns the feel of moving forward. Keep the swimmer's toes flexed out with your hands to ensure good technique. I have the swimmers continue to kick across or down the pool on their own after being launched.

Vertical Kicking

There are two variations of vertical kicking for breaststroke swimmers. One is the traditional vertical kicking in deep water with the arms extended overhead and also with weights in the overhead hands for advanced swimmers. Because vertical kicking decreases the full range of the kicking motion, vertical kicking is a supplementary drill. It requires a nearly continuous kicking action, but it does stress the legs and forces an accelerating kicking movement.

Vertical Kicking at the Wall

The second method of vertical kicking helps to correct a knee-initiated leg recovery. The kick is done in deep water with the swimmer facing and touching the body loosely against the wall. The swimmer kicks with the arms extended overhead, and the wall prevents the swimmer from drawing the knees under the body.

Eggbeater Kicking

Alternating the breaststroke kick from one leg to the other is called the eggbeater kick. This drill helps swimmers attain the very important flexed toe position, and it can be done in the streamlined kicking position or on a kickboard. If a kickboard is used in any of the kicking drills, make certain that it has minimum buoyancy to ensure the most efficient kicking technique.

Arms Behind the Hips Kicking

Have your swimmers lock their thumbs behind the back and as low on the hips as the length of their arms permits. Swimmers are on the frontal position. Have them draw their heels up until they touch their fingertips, before they turn their toes outward for the kick. This action teaches swimmers to bring their heels up behind the buttocks correctly and prevents them from bringing the knees under the body. Swimmers should kick with the head out of the water and the shoulders at water level most of the time in this drill. The swimmer can advance to lowering the head face down in the water at the completion of the kick.

Kicking Breaststroke With a Pull Buoy

Placing a pull buoy between the thighs will help some of your swimmers avoid spreading their knees outward or under on the leg recovery.

Slide/Kick Drill

This drill is designed to teach timing of the arms and legs in breaststroke. Swimmers start from the streamlined kicking position on the front. One hand should be locked over the other. In this position, the hands slide back to the top of the head. The elbows will have to bend to permit this slide of the hands to the head, and the swimmer doesn't kick during this hand slide. Once the hands touch the head, the swimmer lunges forward and kicks. The swimmer must stretch at the completion of the kick before starting the slide of the hands again. At the beginning, have swimmers do only a few strokes without breathing over short distances. As an advanced tech-

nique, you can add breathing to this drill in the following sequence: slide, breathe, lunge, and kick.

OPTIMUM DISTANCE PER STROKE DRILLS

Use these drills and the minimum number drills in the same manner as in the other strokes. Refer to chapter 5.

Feel of the Water

Have your breaststroke swimmers swim with fists only, as indicated for the other strokes. This helps them develop feel for the water, but more importantly, pulling with the fists only in breaststroke speeds up the inward sweep of the arms and the lunge. This can be done dragging the legs or with a dolphin kick.

Also use paddles to develop feel of the water. Changing the size of the paddles and using "naked" paddles without the tubing attachments help the swimmer acquire a feel of the water.

Sculling

Sculling is an extension of feel of the water drills. Refer to chapter 5 for sculling drills and discussion. Swimmers' hands should be high on the water close to the surface in the initial breaststroke scull. The in scull position should also be taught and practiced.

Another more advanced drill is vertical inward sculling. Swimmers take a vertical or standing position in deep water and use only their arms. The in scull movement, also called the "wipe the bowl drill," consists of pressing the hands out a short distance and then sculling in fast. Swimmers press outward to the sides of an imaginary bowl and then down and in along its sides. This sculling will lift them vertically in the water, and the power generated by the in scull becomes obvious to swimmers. Conduct the breaststroke sculling drills with and without paddles.

Gradually build the extended sculling drill to a full arm stroke by using a standing drill in front of the mirror. The walking drill can help teach swimmers to move their body forward on the arm stroke. Use such a drill to move swimmers into a few basic breaststroke arm pulls, with their faces in the water and their legs extended behind them. The swimmers can walk and then push off the bottom and glide forward into this position.

STROKE DRILLS

Pulling With the Head Up

In this drill, swimmers pull with the head up out of the water and with the chin riding on the water surface. Don't use any leg flotation devices in this drill. This teaches swimmers to hold water through both arms' sculls and helps to keep their hands on the water through the stroke. When appropriate, use paddles for some of this pulling.

Pulling With a Flutter Kick

Introducing a flutter kick to the pulling drill and the arm stroke builds on the previous drill. This also helps accelerate the speed of the arms on the in stroke and lunge.

Breaststroke With a Dolphin Kick

This essential breaststroke drill can help swimmers feel the rhythm and have an explosive lunge in breaststroke. Also use fins or monofins in this drill.

Breaststroke Alternating Dolphin and Breaststroke Kick

Have the swimmers perform the breaststroke alternating dolphin and breaststroke kick. The swimmers work down from alternating three kicks dolphin and three kicks of breaststroke to each full stroke, to two of each, and then to one of each.

Inner Tube Pulling

Swimmers can benefit from pulling within an inner tube. If you have swimmers who pull their elbows back behind the shoulder line, place them into a small, passenger car-sized inner tube. The inner tube should rest under their armpits. As they pull breaststroke from this position, the swimmers' arms will bump the inner tube before they can get too far back in the stroke. This self-teaching method reminds the swimmer when to sweep the arms in.

Pulling Over the Lane Line

Swimmers place both arms over the lane line and stroke breaststroke while hanging over the lane line. They should pull from shallow to deeper using the breaststroke body motion.

Swim Under the Rope

Stretch a rope over the water from one end of the pool to the other, preferably over the tops of the starting blocks at the pool's opposite ends. Have your swimmers do the breaststroke under this rope. They should attempt to get enough lift from their in scull to bounce the rope with their head. This power drill for the in scull can help your swimmers feel the wave action.

Surf the Lane Lines

Have the swimmers swim cross-pool by surfing between lane lines. The back of the head, the buttocks, and the heels should all brush the lane line as the swimmer passes under each lane line.

One-Arm Swims

One-arm swims can be done two ways. One method, swimming one-arm breaststroke with one arm extended out front, helps to lengthen the stroke and to maximize the distance per stroke. Have your swimmers keep their forward arm fully extended like a spear. The other method of doing the one-arm breaststroke drill, keeping one arm back at the side, can be used to help some swimmers reduce the amount of their glide.

Shooters

George Block, Alamo Area Aquatics, provides another excellent drill: three right arm pulls, three left arm pulls, and then three both-arm pulls—all with a flutter kick. This increases hand speed on the pull and the lunge.

COMBINATION DRILLS

A combination of various drills is essential for every swimmer. Swimming and teaching breaststroke underwater will help your swimmers achieve a better feel for the stroke. It will also encourage explosive breathing when they surface. For a good variation drill, have your swimmers kick three on the surface in the extended, streamlined arm position and then have them dive underwater and kick three underwater. This combination can also be done in the same manner for pulling and full stroke swimming.

Following are some other examples of combinations: Each segment could be 25 or 50 yards or meters in each of the examples.

1. Torpedo kick on the surface and on the back, torpedo kick on the stomach underwater three kicks, then surface and swim breaststroke, swim breaststroke with dolphin kick, swim breaststroke.

2. Alternate three kicks underwater and three kicks on the surface, three pulls underwater and three pulls on the surface, three strokes underwater and three strokes on the surface, breaststroke at minimum number of strokes.

3. Alternate two dolphin kicks and two breaststroke kicks under and on the surface, alternate breaststroke with a dolphin kick and a breaststroke kick, and then complete two segments of full breaststroke at race pace or maximum speed.

There are numerous combination possibilities. These examples are just the tip of the iceberg. The end result must be more efficient strokes and faster swimming. You have to decide which combination will most benefit your swimmers.

Underwater Pull-Out Drill

Use underwater pull-outs for several strokes or the 25-yard pool length when the swimmers' abilities permit it (see pp. 96-97). Attempt to decrease the number of underwater pull-outs necessary to complete 25 yards.

SUMMARY OF BREASTSTROKE

Use these guidelines to help swimmers attain the technique and subsequent speed necessary for success in breaststroke swimming:

1. The essentials are the same in all breaststroke swimming.
2. The streamlined platform position at the start and finish of each stroke must be attained. The back of the head, spine, and hips must be in line.
3. The out scull is fairly shallow and with the arms extended.
4. The rotation of the arms to the in scull is made by bending the elbows.
5. The anchored position for the in scull is with the elbows up over the hands.
6. The in scull accelerates and finishes about chin level.
7. The swimmer should breathe at the completion of the in scull.
8. The swimmer should lunge forward with the whole body.
9. The kick should be accelerated through the finish.
10. During kicks, heels should be up, knees inside the hip line, and toes outside the knees.

UNDERWATER PULL-OUT DRILL

Position 1

This is the streamlined torpedo position off the wall in preparation for the underwater stroke permitted in breaststroke. Streamline with one hand overlapping the other and the upper arms squeezed tightly behind the ears.

Position 2

This is the long outward scull of the arms that starts the underwater arm pull to maintain the momentum from the dive or turn. The head is facing down.

Position 3

Maintain the elbows as high as possible to anchor on the water and scull the hands inward close to the center line. The head is still facing down and the body should remain close to alignment.

Position 4

Finish the underwater arm pull with a strong push back toward the feet. Streamline with the face down and the back of the head and the spine in alignment. Shrug the shoulders toward the head to streamline as much as possible.

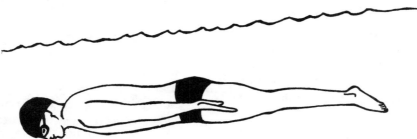

Position 5

Maintain speed from the arm pull by sneaking the arms into the recovery by keeping them close to the body. Simultaneously recover the legs so that the feet and legs are close to staying inside the body line. Begin the kick as the arms pass the shoulders and complete the kick as the arms are extended.

Position 6

Extend the body in a fully streamlined position at the completion of the underwater stroke.

BREASTSTROKE STARTS, TURNS, AND FINISHES

The need to teach and practice starts, turns, and finishes can't be emphasized enough. Swimmers will frequently ask, "When are we going to practice turns?" You need to remind them that they are practicing turns every time they make one in the training session. The same is true for finishes. Every time they touch the wall at the completion of each repeat swim in practice, your swimmers are finishing a race.

You will also have to conduct organized practice on starts, turns, and finishes. Make your practice opportunities count toward great starts, turns, and finishes. This provides a great opportunity to teach and review the basics in these three major areas.

Breaststroke Starts

The basics for the breaststroke start were outlined in chapter 7. The front start information applies to all of the competitive strokes with the exception of backstroke. Some special considerations are unique to the breaststroke starts, because rules permit one full underwater arm pull and kick before the swimmer is required to surface sometime during the second arm stroke. The one underwater arm stroke allowed should be a full pull-through, from the extended position out front to an extended position back on or to the side of the thighs.

Turns

Your swimmers must learn to judge the walls by knowing where the wall is in relation to their stroke from about 15 feet out. Emphasize acceleration into the wall over the last 20 feet or so. It is very important that your swimmers accelerate their last stroke going into the wall, so that they can get high up on the wall for the breaststroke turn. They should avoid coming up to the wall off of a glide on the last stroke, because this will slow their turns.

Swimmers should set their elbows very high on the underwater pull-out, with their hands in under their stomach. They should tuck the shoulders high into the ears at the end of the underwater pull. This hunching action helps to minimize the frontal resistance by reducing eddies between the head and the shoulders.

Swimmers streamline their bodies by keeping their stomach and buttocks in tight and their feet together with the toes pointed. Swimmers should recover their hands close to the body, with the elbows in at their sides.

Have your swimmers start their first surface arm pull after the legs finish the kick. They should snap the feet together and then pull. The first surface stroke starts while the head is still a couple of inches underwater, and it should pop the swimmer through the surface tension. Swimmers should make that first surface stroke very strong. They should break with good momentum and then get into their racing stroke rhythm.

When turning, swimmers should touch the wall just short of their full arm extension. This will allow them to get their feet on the wall faster and to react quicker with their arms to give themselves a faster turn. The lead hand releases from the wall on contact, with the elbow down. The other hand grips or pushes, depending on whether the wall is flat or has a gutter to assist in getting the legs to the wall. Swimmers should drive their knees into their chest as quickly as possible. The elbow of the first arm off the wall goes down quickly, with the hand facing upward toward the ceiling. Swimmers should use this hand to scoop water up quickly, because it will get their legs on the wall faster. The feet should be crossed, one on top of the other, to help bring them to the wall through one hole in the water and not two. This action will help the swimmer get to the wall quicker.

The second hand off the wall comes close to the ear for the push-off. Your swimmers should come out through the same hole in the water that they made going into the wall. The eyes should be focused on the turning point of the wall going in and then should move to the

TURNS

Position 1

Make the touch on the wall just short of full arm extension for a quicker turn.

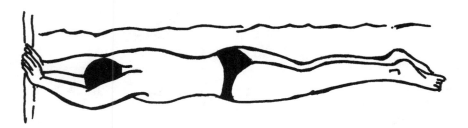

Position 2

One hand releases the wall on contact with the elbow leading. Drive the knees into the chest quickly with the lead hand sculling upward to whip the legs into the wall. Cross the feet, one of top of the other, to lessen resistance and get the feet on the wall faster.

Position 3

The second hand comes off the wall close to the ear for the push-off. The eye position moves to the vertical for the push-off. Attempt to come off the wall through the same hole in the water that was made going into the wall.

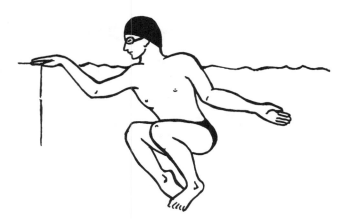

Position 4

Extend the streamlined body off the wall and then go into the underwater stroke as indicated in the underwater pull-out drill.

vertical position as the second arm comes off the wall. This will help your swimmers get in and out through one hole. They should extend the entire body into a streamlined position off the wall and then go into the underwater stroke and the breakout as indicated in the start section.

Finishes

Teach your swimmers to finish their breaststroke races with both arms fully extended on the surface and with their faces and eyes looking down in the water. Each swimmer's body should be in one straight line. Swimmers should make a determined lunge on their final stroke to get their hands on the wall as fast as possible. Provide special time for swimmers to practice this skill.

SUMMARY FOR BREASTSTROKE STARTS, TURNS, AND FINISHES

1. Instruct swimmers to set the elbows high on the underwater pull-out.
2. Swimmers should hunch the shoulders at the completion of this pull-out.
3. On turns, swimmers should touch the wall just short of full extension.
4. Fast turns depend on getting the feet on the wall quickly.
5. Swimmers should finish with both arms fully extended.

Chapter 10

BUTTERFLY

The simultaneous dolphin kick in butterfly swimming is explained in chapter 6. Refer to chapter 6 for butterfly kicking technique tips and teaching drills.

The butterfly arm stroke is also done simultaneously, and the stroke is done on the front without body rotation. It is a short-axis stroke, as is breaststroke. Consider the technique that you want to teach first; then use the sequence of skill drills that will teach it most effectively.

TECHNICAL ASPECTS

You will need to teach technique that maximizes propulsion and distance per stroke and minimizes resistance. Swimmers can learn the butterfly as easily as any other competitive stroke when you are confident in your teaching skills. You are the key.

Expect quality butterfly at all times in practice. Permitting the stroke to break down and then allowing swimmers to practice it imperfectly aren't recommended. There are five areas of consideration for your coaching: entry, arm pull, recovery, kicking, and breathing.

Entry

Teach your swimmers to reach long on the entry. They will get good distance on their stroke by extending the arms and body on entry. The arms should be thrown to the other end of the pool. The head should be down on entry landing. This will help the

BUTTERFLY

Position 1

The extended "platform" position is illustrated. The back of the head and spine are in line and the face is looking forward. The hands are pitched with the thumbs slightly down.

Position 2

The hands are making the catch and the arms are cocked slightly to anchor the elbows on the water.

Position 3

The hands are at mid-pull with the wrists slightly flexed to enable the hands to continue to push water back. The head and trunk are moving toward the breakout.

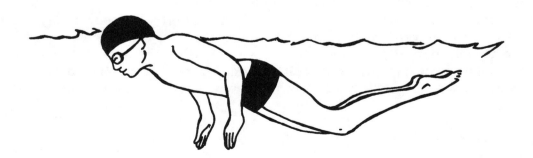

Position 4

The hands are finishing the stroke in the "front end" butterfly. The hands are beginning to move away and to the outside ("hands away").

Position 5

The breath is taken at the finish of the stroke and start of the recovery. The eyes are looking at an angle to the water. This is a leaning position toward the water to avoid a high head and increased resistance of the stroke.

Position 6

The head and face are dropping down again so that the arms and head can land simultaneously.

Position 7

The platform landing features the arms, head, and spine in alignment.

swimmers get their arms into the entry quickly and efficiently. The result is a flat back on entry. The back of the head and the spine must be aligned, so that the kick will spear a streamlined body forward.

It is very important that the back of the head and the spine are lined up during this entry position. Swimmers must keep the face down in the water and the head aligned with the spine. The face and chest are pressed down and forward. It helps to have the eyes focus down and only slightly forward. Everything lands at once, and this brings the hips up on the water. The timing is to have the hips up high on the arm entry and the face down with the legs fully extended.

The back of the head and the spine must be lined up during the entry position.

I used to tell swimmers to throw the head to the chest just before the arm entry. This gave the necessary timing, but it also placed the head lower than the spine. Use some caution and adjust the head throw to allow swimmers more control and to keep their heads and spines aligned. I call this the "hinged" position with the head and spine hinged. This will give swimmers a longer body on the water in the best position to take advantage of the coming arm stroke.

Water should cover the back of the head and spine after entry. There is an underwater portion to this stroke, and one of the best ways to see it is to watch swimmers upside-down: On the deck, bend over and watch them looking back under your armpit.

Butterfly swimmers should enter the water at a point just inside the shoulders to the armpit width to eliminate much of the resistance encountered when arms enter wide of the shoulder. It also permits a more continuous and fluid butterfly because the hands are in good position to start the arm stroke. Entering with arms too close together delays the swimmer getting into the catch and stroke cleanly.

Arm Pull

I learned a "front end" butterfly stroke from Howard Firby of Canada almost 40 years ago. It is only recently that some coaches are again advocating front end butterfly. The distinguishing characteristic is that the emphasis is on setting up a great front end on the stroke, and the swimmer avoids taking the stroke too far back into a push phase finish of the stroke. It is a longer stroke out front and decreases resistance. I have always believed in this butterfly technique, and it will be my model in this chapter.

The front end butterfly features an early in scull of the hands after a short out scull to set up the catch. The hands almost touch on this in scull at a position from under the chin to the upper chest just under the shoulder level.

The outward scull finishing the stroke must be timed correctly for each swimmer. The push and outward finish of the stroke are called "hands away" or "karate exit." Pushing the water too far back won't permit a clean exit of the arm stroke and discourages front end butterfly. The outward scull blends the back, out, and up hand movement with the emphasis on hands away at the finish. This finish of the stroke, or exit, is somewhere between the navel and upper hips. The little fingers lead the hands away into the recovery.

Recovery

The hands-away exit creates momentum into the recovery. The arms will maintain the extended arm position on exit into the recovery. The emphasis is on relaxed arms in the recovery. The arms are again thrown toward the other end of the pool. Teach swimmers to always reach long out front. The face should be lowered toward the water as the arms are moving toward the entry. The arms and head should land on the water at the same time.

Kicking

To swim faster butterfly, the swimmer needs to kick faster. This is the goal in dolphin kicking. To keep the butterfly kick continuous and explosive, it must originate from the hips with flexible knees, as it does in the crawl (see chapter 6). There should be two kicks to every arm cycle. One kick should be delivered on the landing of the head and arms on the water in the front end of the stroke. The second kick comes at the end of the underwater arm stroke in the hands-away phase.

Breathing

Teach swimmers to breathe late in the arm pull. They should begin to move the chin forward toward the breathing position on the final push and hands-away section of the arm stroke. Breathing can occur at the end of the hands-away exit and start of the recovery. This is the most efficient position in which to breathe, because the swimmer's shoulders are out of the water. Swimmers should learn to breathe without focusing on lifting the head or chin but should attempt to relax and lean forward with the chin resting on the water.

Teach swimmers to breathe on every second stroke, even though many great butterfly swimmers can breathe every stroke efficiently. You can sort this out later as your swimmers mature. The 200-yard butterfly races may require breathing every stroke at times for some swimmers to be successful. However, if you teach breathing every other stroke, you'll make many of the other skills easier to learn. The head must remain hinged to the spine on the nonbreathing stroke for an efficient butterfly.

Side breathing is a viable option for many swimmers. I've taught a number of side breathers. The principles of breathing remain the same, although some emphasis must be placed on swimming a straight line with side breathers.

Sequence of Teaching Butterfly

Teach or review the torpedo position first. This is the landing position of front end butterfly. It is a matter of personal preference whether you teach the dolphin kick next or begin with the arms.

My personal preference is usually to teach the arm stroke first. You can teach the arms and legs almost simultaneously, but I prefer that swimmers feel they are actually swimming butterfly before I introduce the leg action.

After you have taught the basic arm stroke, proceed to the torpedo butterfly. The streamlined torpedo body is the basic out front position for the stroke. Have swimmers push off the wall for a review of the torpedo position used in crawl. Swimmers should be only one body width under the surface when in the torpedo position. Next they repeat this from a push-off and glide, and when the swimmer begins to slow down, he or she should scull out with the hands, take one butterfly arm stroke, and throw the arms out front returning to the torpedo position. Even if it is only one stroke, this is butterfly.

Swimmers should get their arms back into the water in the extended torpedo position quietly. Playing a game with beginners is effective. Close your eyes, turn your back to the swimmers, and challenge them to make a stroke that you can't hear. They can add a second stroke after they again attain that torpedo or dead man's position in subsequent attempts.

The kicking drills of chapter 6 should be taught at least by this point of the learning process if they weren't introduced after the torpedo body position.

I advise coming back to the arm stroke with a one-arm drill that is built from the kicking drills. I would then work breathing drills into the one-arm drills, using an orderly and natural sequence. Finally, add any number of butterfly drills to maximize distance per stroke before introducing any timed swims.

Don't permit your swimmers to breathe on the first arm pull. They can breathe on the second stroke or later depending on the distance of the race and their personal preference. On the first stroke, swimmers should exaggerate the hands-away ("karate") finish off the underwater stroke and to get into the recovery. This first arm stroke is actually a little shorter than the subsequent strokes. This helps the swimmer to get into front end butterfly cleanly. Stress a very clean entry on this first arm stroke, because it requires great streamlining and maximizes the momentum swimmers receive from their start and into the early butterfly strokes.

SPECIAL TIPS FOR TEACHING THE BUTTERFLY

The sequence of the major training drills is important. Particularly in the case of butterfly, all drills must be done correctly, because butterfly swimmers suffer the most from poor technique. Good technique makes this stroke easy and a work of art. There is beauty in good butterfly swimming, but the beast appears quickly when the stroke breaks down into bad butterfly technique.

Swimmers should practice butterfly drills and swimming for distances within their skill level, because their stroke will break down if you overload them. Perfect technique in practice is your goal.

Optimum Distance Per Stroke

Maximum distance per stroke drills must be done in butterfly as they were done in the other strokes. Counting strokes per length is the basic drill. You must also use the minimum number drills. Refer to chapter 5 for these drills.

Feel of the Water

Butterfly drills and swimming with only the clenched fist will help swimmers to attain better feel of the water. Alternating the clenched fist with an open or partially open hand is recommended. I favor the use of my own holed paddles, Han's Paddles, to gain better feel and hold on the water. This particular paddle is small enough to fit to the form of the hand, and the large numbers of holes permit water flow through the paddle onto the hand. It permits the swimmer to attain a good hold on the water without increasing the risk of joint injury.

Fins

I prefer to use the shortened fins and the "shooter" monofins for these kicking drills. Fins can be used in almost all of the kicking and swimming drills, but consider them necessary in teaching the dolphin kick.

Paddle Swims

I already described how important Han's Paddles are in a swimmer's attempt to improve the feel of the water. The size and shape of the hand-sized black holed paddle (the Han's Paddle) are ideally suited for butterfly swimming.

A larger paddle should be used only by more mature swimmers and only in special situations. I designed two other paddles, the Groover and the Gripper, that are larger. These paddles make the swimmer aware of a clean hands-away exit and a clean entry. The paddles will catch water and be difficult to keep on the hand when the swimmer is inefficient during the hand exit and entry.

I recommend using Han's Paddles in the short power swims. I use them almost exclusively in our power rack swims and often in short power bursts. I also use them in race-pace swims to help swimmers optimize their distance per stroke.

Distance and Endurance Considerations

The racing distance in butterfly extends to 200 (yards or meters), which is not a long race. Some butterfly swimmers might argue that point, but those who develop great butterfly technique can swim the 200.

A powerful leg kick is essential for success in the butterfly, particularly for the 100 butterfly swimmer. In the 200, swimmers may breathe more often than every two strokes to finish well. Sustained speed is more important in the 200, so optimizing the distance per stroke drills is essential.

Basic Arms

If you can effectively reach and hold their arms through the full stroke, you should get into the water with your younger swimmers, stand behind them, and work their arms manually.

In front of a wall mirror, have your swimmers do the standing drill in waist-deep water. If you don't have a mirror, have them face you and duplicate the butterfly arm stroke that you are doing on the pool deck. Fix and hold certain arm stroke positions and talk them through each one.

1. Arms enter at just inside the shoulder width.

2. Hands should be pitched out on entry with the little finger higher than the thumb.

3. Fingertips should be pointed down and elbow anchored over the hands.

4. Hands rotate in and almost touch under the chin or upper chest.

5. The swimmer should perform a hands-away or karate exit between the navel and upper hips.

6. Arms should be thrown long and forward.

7. Arms and head should land together out front.

Next swimmers should do the walking butterfly drill into and away from the mirror. Then move swimmers from the walking butterfly to one or two strokes of butterfly without breathing.

DRILLS FOR THE BUTTERFLY

Always explain each skill, demonstrate it correctly, and then have swimmers practice it within the particular drill you are teaching.

Jumping Jack Butterfly

I use this drill for beginners. I don't consider it to be essential, but many coaches use it and young kids love to do it. In waist-deep water, the swimmer leaps off the bottom and dives through the surface, goes back underwater, and then repeats the process.

One-Arm Swims With One Arm Extended

Variations of one-arm swims are the backbone of learning the butterfly, but the first step is to learn the one-arm butterfly with one arm extended. Through the full stroke cycle, the arm must be speared forward and fully extended with the little finger pitched slightly up. The swimmer should breathe to the side in this drill, on the side of the stroking arm.

Breathing to the stroking arm side automatically teaches the swimmer to breathe late in the pull. As the arm finishes the stroke, the shoulder lifts and the chin can easily follow the shoulder to breathe. Have swimmers practice this drill on both sides.

The next step is to move from the one-arm stroke to the full stroke. I usually start with a 3/3/3 drill. Swimmers do three one-arm butterfly strokes on the right side and breathe to the right, then swim three one-arm strokes on the left side and breathe to the left, and then swim three full butterfly strokes and breathe forward every second stroke. This drill teaches the breathing timing and the rhythm of butterfly. Moving from side breathing to forward breathing establishes the late pattern for butterfly.

My next combined drill is a 1/1/1, 1/1/2, 1/1/3, and so on. Swimmers do one butterfly stroke on the right side, one on the left, and then one full butterfly stroke. Immediately they go back to one stroke on the right, one on the left, and two full butterfly strokes, and then so on, to whatever number of full strokes that you desire according to the swimmers' level.

Once swimmers learn these one-arm drills, you can improvise any challenging combination, like three right arm strokes, two left, one right, three left. An example combination drill for your more advanced swimmers would be three right arm strokes with breathing on the right side, three full butterfly strokes with no breathing, three left arm strokes with breathing on the left side, and three full strokes with no breathing.

Multiple Kick Butterfly

For this drill swimmers do the full stroke, but they kick three, four, or five or more kicks, with the arms speared out front, before they take their next stroke. This drill encourages front end butterfly and a fast, strong kick. I like to combine this multiple kicking drill with the torpedo back butterfly kick. For example, when swimming 50s, athletes do the first 25 in five-kick butterfly and the last in torpedo back butterfly kick.

Another variation of this drill is to do five kicks underwater and then two explosive full strokes of swimming. Challenge your swimmers with new variations in these drills, but always demand perfect technique.

Extra Kicks Off Walls

Kicking five or more times off each wall before breaking out into the arm stroke is a good drill to teach swimmers to use explosive kicking. Swimmers should streamline their bodies into a full torpedo position through all of these kicks. The extra kicks also help to establish the importance of the kick off every wall and will assist the swimmer in determining his or her best underwater kicking distance. Current rules limit this to a maximum of 15 meters.

One-Arm Swims With One Arm at the Side

In this drill, swimmers do one-arm butterfly with the nonstroking arm at the side. This shortens the swimmer's stroke slightly and eliminates some of the glide out front on the entry.

Vertical Butterfly

The swimmer stands vertically with the arms extended overhead in deep water and slightly submerged. The swimmer takes one butterfly stroke and kicks to the highest point possible out of the water.

Sculling

As in all strokes, emphasize sculling. The sculling drills outlined in chapter 5 are essential in butterfly.

Transition Drills

Using a sequence of drills that combine and lead into the full stroke is a very efficient method of teaching. There is no limit to the combinations that are available. Following are some examples (all of the examples could be done with or without fins or hand paddles):

1. The swimmer starts with 25 yards back torpedo dolphin kick with a rotation to the front that allows two full butterfly strokes, then 25 front torpedo dolphin kick and surface for three full butterfly strokes. This drill could continue, building the number of full strokes each 25. It could also be done in crossed arm kicking instead of the streamlined torpedo kick.

2. The swimmer does 25 kick underwater on the side or front with fins or monofins, 25 back dolphin kick on the surface, 25 with five underwater kicks, and the remainder in full stroke.

3. The swimmer does 25 four-kick butterfly stroke, 25 back dolphin kick on the surface, 25 of three right and then three left arm strokes, and then three full butterfly strokes. The swimmer should breathe to the side on the single-arm strokes and breathe front on the full strokes.

4. The swimmer does 25 crawl arm stroke with dolphin kick; 25 crawl arm stroke in the same way as the first 25 but with the head up; 25 of a single right arm, and then the left arm butterfly, followed by two full butterfly strokes (repeat but add one additional butterfly stroke in each subsequent sequence); and 25 full butterfly swimming. Fins are recommended on this progression.

5. The swimmer repeats 100s with five kicks underwater off each wall; 25 of three left arm, then three right arm butterfly, and three full strokes; and 25 of full stroke butterfly. Then the swimmer repeats the same sequence on the next 2 × 25. Count the strokes on the 25s of full stroke swimming.

Speed Drill

In the torpedo position, swimmers kick six to eight fast power kicks underwater and then break out with three very fast and full butterfly strokes before returning to regular pace. Another speed drill involves swimming short bursts—any distance from 10 to 20 yards, depending on the swimmer's ability—of no-breath sprints on longer rest and perfect stroke.

SUMMARY OF BUTTERFLY

These are the guidelines for teaching and coaching great butterfly:

1. Teach and expect quality butterfly.
2. Teach swimmers to reach long out front on entry.
3. Have swimmers enter near the armpits just inside the shoulders.
4. On entry, the swimmer's palms should be down and pitched out slightly.
5. Swimmers should scull or press out to just outside the shoulders.
6. Swimmers should anchor the elbows over the hands.
7. Teach swimmers to scull inward and build arm speed to a point under the belly button.
8. Have them breathe late in the stroke during the karate exit.
9. Swimmers should use hands-away or a karate exit.
10. The exit and start of the recovery involve little fingers leading.

11. The head and arms should enter out front at the same time.
12. On entry, the back of the head and spine are aligned.
13. Butterfly should be partially done underwater.
14. Swimmers should practice at distances that maintain quality technique.
15. Teach swimmers to breathe every second stroke.

BUTTERFLY STARTS, TURNS, AND FINISHES

Follow my same recommendations for the other strokes. Teach and practice starts, turns, and finishes, because your swimmers will never get consistently fast unless you provide the necessary techniques and the time to practice them.

Butterfly Starts

The front start discussed in chapter 7 provides the basics for all front starts; however, there are some special considerations for the butterfly start. Before breaking out into the arm stroke, swimmers must establish the kick underwater with very quick and shallow butterfly kicks while streamlining in the torpedo position. Present rules allow up to 15 meters underwater before the swimmer breaks into the arm strokes. This is also true in crawl starts, but a greater percentage of butterfly swimmers have the dolphin kick proficiency to take full advantage of this rule. For these swimmers, underwater is faster!

Turns

The butterfly turn is the same as the breaststroke turn at the wall. (For specifics, refer to the turn section of chapter 9.) Once the push-off has been executed, the same special considerations that I have already indicated for the butterfly apply to the turn. Judging the wall is critical for the success of the butterfly turn, as it is in the breaststroke.

The no-wall drill in midpool helps teach fast butterfly turns. Have your swimmers do three very fast strokes to midpool, and then have them turn quickly without the wall and repeat.

Finishes

The swimmer must have both arms fully extended and the head down in the aligned position. No breathing from the backstroke flags to the finish is the rule. Swimmers must judge the wall correctly. It may be necessary to kick and reach when another stroke will be detrimental. Getting the hands on the wall fast is a learned skill, and swimmers must practice it.

A Golden Touch

I interviewed on video several of the finalists in the butterfly events at the 1992 Olympic Trials for my presentation at the American Swimming Coaches' Association World Clinic. Several months prior to the Olympic Games, Pablo Morales told me about all the time he spent practicing the butterfly race finish and about how he would focus on making a good finish when he was tired at the race's end. Pablo Morales won a very close 100-meter butterfly race and the gold medal at Barcelona as a result of his practice.

SUMMARY OF BUTTERFLY STARTS, TURNS, AND FINISHES

1. Whenever it is advantageous, use the 15 meters allowed underwater in the dolphin kick off the start and turns.
2. Swimmers must not breathe on the first arm pull off the walls.
3. The butterfly turn is the same as the breaststroke turn.
4. A correctly timed finish will win races.

Part III

COACHING PLANS

Chapter
11

PLANNING TRAINING

I always began planning for the next high school season within a few days after a state championship meet. "Failure to plan is planning to fail." I also began planning for the next year after the club season's national championship.

Every year that I coached, I tried to live by the philosophy, "To be satisfied is to be finished." As I have stated, for me, planning always starts soon after the season-ending championship meet, even a very successful state championship meet. At that time, everything is in its proper perspective to evaluate the past season and begin to plan for the next. I always ask myself, "What went well and what went wrong?"

DEVELOPING YOUR PLAN

A written plan will chart your course for the coming year or longer. Your swimmers commit more readily to a long-range plan when they see it in print, and you need to have a guiding road map. Planning allows me to commit myself to my best effort over any given time period.

The Planning Time Period

The time period for which you plan can be for the few months of a short high school season, for the full year, or for an even longer period of time. Typically, for the most success, you should plan for the full school year as a high school coach.

As a club coach, I planned for one full year. Club coaches will have a minimum of two competitive seasons, the short-course and the long-course seasons, within a year. Short course, usually in the fall and winter, is in 25-yard and 25-meter pools. Long course, in the spring and summer, is in 50-meter pools.

Some club coaches will plan for the three-season year. The third season occurs in fall and has a championship meet designed to attain the time standards necessary to enter the championship meets of the short- and long-course seasons, which come later in the year.

A quadrennial, or four-year, plan is designed to lead into each Olympic Games. National teams and some elite athletes will train under a quadrennial plan specifically to reach their peak performance level for the Olympic Games.

The Ingredients of a Plan

Your plan should include the following components of preseason conditioning, the competitive season, the postseason transition, and breaks.

1. Dry land cross-training
2. Increases in distance and intensity of the training
3. Basic technique skills
4. Motivational methods necessary for success
5. Amount and frequency of speed work
6. Special drills for starts, turns, finishes, and relay exchanges
7. Amount and frequency of race pace and endurance training
8. Length and requirements of the taper, or peak preparation

You should plan the transition from high school swimming to club swimming when you are the high school coach, including encouraging your high school swimmers to report to their club coach immediately after their high school season. You should provide the club coach with your swimmers' best training times and their championship meet results.

Similarly, when you are the club coach, you should plan the transition from club swimming to high school swimming. You need to work out a training plan with the high school coach. Your swimmers may continue to swim some club meets during the high school season, depending on the interscholastic rules in your state. As club coach, you've known your swimmers for a long time, so inform the high school coach about their best events, their training habits, and whatever else can help ease the transition.

It may be mutually agreeable that the club swimmer continue to train, at least as often as possible, with the club coach to ensure training continuity. A common model is for the swimmer to compete for the high school but train with the club and high school during the high school season. The club and high school coaches should collaborate to accommodate their particular situation.

As a club coach, you need to recognize the value of high school swimming. Your swimmers have a good opportunity to excel on a high school team. The competition in high school swimming is more localized, which can be good and bad news. The good news is when a swimmer gains the confidence and the motivation to step up into increased competition at the club level. The bad news is that the swimmer might become satisfied to excel at the high school level only and fail to challenge him- or herself to reach another level.

Also, high school sports receive more media coverage, so good swimmers get recognized. High school swimming also places a special emphasis on speed, which can help develop your swimmers in that important area.

On the other hand, if you're a high school coach, you should recognize that club swimming provides for elite swimming opportunities. The path to national and international competition is through USA Swimming. Year-round training opportunities and multiple distances in every stroke are the reality of club swimming. Emphasis on more events and longer distances in all strokes in club swimming makes the club swimmer the nucleus of a successful high school team.

A Statistical Fact

With a few exceptions, the swimmers who win and place at the state high school championship meets are almost always year-round club swimmers. I have worked with individual event high school state champions who had not been club members prior to high school but who became club swimmers in order to win. This is a fact in swimming, so you should plan accordingly.

The Master Calendar

Make a master calendar and list your schedule of competition as the first step. Build everything else around this meet schedule.

Which meets are important and how important? Which is the most significant meet that your team will enter during that season? It was always the state championship meet for our Wilson High School team that determined the success of our team.

The USA Swimming Senior National Championship meet would ideally be the most significant meet for our Tacoma Swim Club. Every fourth year the Olympic Trials would become our most important competition.

For grassroots swim clubs, the meet most important would likely be a championship meet prior to the Senior National Championship, because the great majority are developmental clubs. Most clubs will have too few swimmers who qualify for a Senior National Championship to make a legitimate run at winning at that level.

Only the Elite Qualify

Tacoma Swim Club has had many swimmers score and even win at the Senior National Championship meet, and we placed teams in the top 10 several times. However, the number of qualifiers for the national championship was usually small. The size of our national team entry has varied from one to the middle teens. The average size of those teams qualifying to attend the Senior National Championship is only two or three swimmers, which is too few for a significant team finish.

Our most important team championship will more often be the association, sectionals, zone, or Junior National Championship meet when it is offered.

You should indicate which meets are important enough to require some rest and designate which swimmers on the team should rest. Stress the importance of the goal championship meet as the culmination of all your efforts in previous competitions. Here is where your swimmers should record their best performances.

Listing your competitive schedule is a first step. You can add the daily training sessions and the vacation training schedule to a monthly plan that is more inclusive. List the major school functions, such as formal dances and the semester final exam days as well, because you need to know when outside pressure is the greatest on your swimmers.

A Foreign Example

I had a close friend, Dave Haller, who at one time was the national coach for Hong Kong. He was from Great Britain, and most of his swimmers were from Chinese families. He soon became aware of the cultural differences of his Hong Kong swimmers. For one thing, his swimmers would cease to come to practice for about three weeks during final exam time. Dave soon learned that they made class work their number one priority, and he planned accordingly after his first year.

Aerobic Training Provides the Foundation

Dennis Pursley, former national team director for USA Swimming, provided the following quotation. "Many coaches have long believed that a strong aerobic foundation of endurance training during the developmental years is essential to maximum potential development for most swimmers, including sprinters, from a career perspective. Although this hypothesis continues to be debated today, it is still strongly supported by statistics, anecdotal evidence, and scientific research. It seems to especially hold true for long course performances. Advanced technology is becoming more and more prevalent in our sport; but teamwork, strength of character, and a strong work ethic continue to be the cornerstones of success."

This has been the basic premise of my coaching and training plans as well, and it continues at Tacoma Swim Club.

A strong aerobic foundation of endurance training during the developmental years is essential to maximum potential development for most swimmers, including sprinters, from a career perspective.

PLANNING THE YEARLY CLUB TRAINING SCHEDULE

Planning centers on training. Jay Benner replaced me as the head coach of Tacoma Swim Club on my retirement. I have continued to be a volunteer part-time coach with Jay. He has produced the current women's 100-meter long-course national champion, and she had a second place in the 200-meter butterfly. In addition, a 13-year-old boy has set a new national short-course age-group record for 3,000-yard freestyle, with a time of 30:01.15. Both of these swimmers excelled at distances of 100 meters up through 3,000 yards, and they participated in very similar training.

Jay's program is constructed around aerobic-based endurance training. His background as a swimmer was in the 400 individual medley and the 1,500 freestyle. He eventually was on the USA Swimming National Open Water Marathon Team. He still swims in professional marathon swims throughout the world. His experiences have honed his belief in aerobic-based training. His outline of the Tacoma Swim Club season plan is the model presented here.

TWO-SEASON YEARLY PLAN

The short-course season runs from mid-September to April, a period of 28 to 30 weeks. The long-course season extends from April to mid-August, 18 to 20 weeks. The segments of the swimming year beginning in September are as follows:

General Endurance

The goal of general endurance is to improve the overall aerobic and fitness levels of each swimmer. This segment is for 10 weeks. The emphasis is on EN1, kicking, and stroke drills. Individual medley training is emphasized along with resistance training with parachutes and buckets (the equipment is explained in chapter 12; EN1 and the other training categories are explained later in this chapter).

Starting in week 4, threshold training is gradually introduced and is about 20% of the total volume over the next six weeks. Sprint training is minimal during this period, but a small amount is done daily and not more than 5 percent of the weekly total. Pulling with tubes in EN1 is done daily and amounts to about 20 percent of the weekly total. The remainder of the water training is EN1. Running is done three times a week for 30 to 40 minutes over the first six weeks of the general endurance segment. Morning training starts during week 3 of the short-course season and in week 2 of the long-course season.

Specific Endurance

This segment takes place during eight weeks. The goal is to improve aerobic endurance and to maximize the anaerobic threshold. The emphasis is on each swimmer's specialty events. The weekly volume peaks during the final weeks of this specific endurance phase. During the short-course season, the peak training load occurs during winter holiday vacation. The training volume is overloaded for one and a half to two weeks with three sessions per day. During the long-course season, this period occurs the last one and a half weeks of June into the first one and a half weeks of July. The difference in the long-course season is that three sessions per day are conducted on only two days a week, Tuesdays and Thursdays, but for three weeks.

After the overload training is completed, the volume is dropped back to the levels prior to the overload. However, the training intensity is increased. The goal is to produce supercompensation, which works well going into the anaerobic phase. Threshold swimming makes up about 25 percent of the total volume, except in the overload phase where it drops back to 15 percent. Speed training is gradually increased and makes up about 10 percent of the weekly volume. The middle-distance and sprint swimmers do approximately 10 percent less total volume than the distance swimmers during the last four to five weeks of this specific endurance phase.

Anaerobic and Competition Phase

This segment is six to eight weeks in length. The goal is to develop speed and focus on race-pace training while maintaining aerobic fitness. The shift is to an anaerobic emphasis for the sprinters and the middle-distance swimmers. Lactate training and power training are introduced.

The sprinting is increased for the 200 events and shorter distances. Distance swimmers focus on race pace as well as threshold and overload training. Morning training sessions are decreased for sprinters and are usually moderate with a few sprints included. Three or four meets are scheduled during this training period. Weekly mileage volumes are gradually decreased throughout this phase.

Rest and Peak Preparation

This phase usually lasts from two to four weeks. The goal is to permit adaptation for peak performance levels. The volume and intensity are reduced. This special preparation is explained in chapter 13.

Supplemental Considerations

The long-course season is set up to include shortened phases of general and specific endurance. Each of these segments is reduced to six weeks. Aerobic fitness is at a higher level at the end of the short-course season than at the start. Lactate production sets start in week 4 of the long-course season on a regular basis.

Timed 3,000 test swims are done four or five times during the short-course season and three times during the long-course season. This measures the anaerobic threshold levels and the progress being made in adaptation to the training. The goal is to improve the anaerobic threshold.

Subthreshold swimming is done frequently throughout the season. This involves swimming at approximately two seconds per 100 slower than threshold pace. This method helps the swimmer progress to fast swimming but with controlled effort.

Swimming categories are explained in table 11.1. EN1 can be practiced in long swims or repeats with a short rest interval of 10 to 30 seconds, depending on the distance of the repeats. The 100s would be at the short end of the rest interval, 10 seconds, for example. These are done at subthreshold speed. EN2 is usually conducted in repeat swims with a short rest interval of 10 to 30 seconds, depending on the distance of the repeats. EN2 can also be done in long swims such as a 3,000, which is often the test distance for determining aerobic threshold pace for individual swimmers. These are at threshold speed. EN3 is in repeat swims with a longer rest interval of 20 seconds to a 1:1 ratio. This maximal effort is about 5 to 7 percent faster than the threshold pace.

SP1 is done inside of 90 percent maximum velocity, or personal best times. The work–rest ratio is at least 1:1 or 1:2, or even more. SP2 is inside of 95 percent maximum velocity. The work-rest ratio is at least 1:2 and could go much higher, such as 1:8. SP3 is 100 percent and faster

Table 11.1 Training Categories

				USA Swimming Energy Categories	
Cat	System	HR	Lactate	General/specific	Emphasis
REC	na	na	na	na	Drills, recovery swims
EN1	aerobic	120-140	0 to 2	Overall general, increase in stroke volume, improves capillary network and transport of energy, improves fat metabolism	Perfect technique, DPS efficiency
EN2	aerobic	140-160	1 to 4	Effect specific to working muscle. Enhances steady state where lactate is removed and used as fast as produced.	Perfect technique, DPS efficiency
EN3	aerobic	160-max	4 to 10	Both general and specific effects. General: Max O_2 uptake and delivery to working muscle. Specific: Both removal rates and levels of tolerance of lactic acid in the working muscle.	Technique, DPS efficiency
SP1	anaerobic	max	8 to 16	Both general and specific. General: Improves delivery of energy through anaerobic sources. Improves pain threshold. Specific: Improves buffering capacity of the working muscles. Improves lactic acid tolerance in the working muscles.	The emphasis shifts away from technique work and more toward racing and challenging the athletes. Criteria and order of importance: speed, tempo, stroke count, and heart rate.
SP2	anaerobic	max	max	Specific: Max lactate production. High end tolerance and buffering capacity.	Emphasis is on racing skills. Criteria: speed and tempo.
SP3	anaerobic	na	1 to 3	Specific: Enhances usage creatine pool by the working muscle.	Perfect technique at max velocity for short distances. As the season progresses, this should become race tempo specific.

Note: na = not applicable; DPS = distance per stroke

than maximum velocity. The distances are short, less than 25 yards. The rest ratio should be about 1:2, but it can be shorter, for example, 4 (4 × 12-1/2 yards). The 4 × 12-1/2 can be done with only a couple seconds of rest, but each set of four has a rest interval of at least 1:2.

The energy categories overlap one another within training sets. One example would be descending swims, such as 9 × 400, descending 1 to 3, with EN1 in Swim 1, EN2 in Swim 2, and EN3 in Swim 3. Each team member may train in a slightly different category than other team members within any particular set. This is the result of the different ability levels on the team and the individual training adaptation taking effect. Each training set has a desired energy category response, and it will take experience and insight by the coach to hit the desired energy level goal.

Following are some examples of training sets for each energy category: EN1—Pulling with a tube; 20 × 50, alternating two 50s in drill and two 50s build swim; cruise effort 15 × 200 yards on 2:30 maintaining a 130-beat heart rate. EN2—Swimming sets at aerobic threshold pace, a set total of 2,500 to 3,500, such as 30 × 100 on a send-off that allows about a 10-second rest interval. EN3—Swimming sets at faster than threshold with slightly more rest such as 15 × 200 yards on 2:30, assuming the EN3 speed would permit 20 or more seconds of rest.

SP1—Fast swims that are inside of 10 percent slower than personal best swims; 8 × 100 on 2:00. SP2—Very fast swims that are inside of 5 percent slower than personal best swims; 16 × dive 50 on 2:00, two 50s at SP2 followed by one 50 at recovery. SP3—Short swims faster than race pace of the personal best swims. Cross-pool: Kick set 8 (4 × 15 or pool width) very fast on 15 seconds. Kick torpedo dolphin underwater on the odd and torpedo back flutter on the even. Rest 30 seconds between sets, SP3. Swim set: Cross-pool sprints: Sprint 4 (4 × 15) on 10 seconds, 45 seconds rest between each set of 4 × 15, in major stroke.

When developing your training schedule, you must ensure that the appropriate levels of training intensity are provided throughout the season. This is the cycle that you build into your training calendar. Insert drills, kick-ing, pulling, starts, turns, finishes, relay exchanges, and whatever else you believe is necessary within this guideline. Adjust your yardage goals to accommodate the pool time available, the specific event needs, and the swimming background of each team member.

Be prepared to adjust your planning from year to year or season to season. Changing your plan is necessary, because your experiences will lead to new knowledge and scientific research may provide new information. You will review your plan at the end of each season, and this information often dictates change. This is part of the process of keeping the challenge in each new swimming year.

No one training program is ever going to be the best forever. I believe that the training program should be individualized for particular strokes, distance of the event, and swimmers. My suggestions are guidelines to build upon.

The Australian training system incorporates heart rate control with fast race pace and speed swimming. Ron Johnson, the retired Arizona State swim coach, calls this "easy speed" swimming. Swimming sets that are at race pace and a sustainable heart rate level would classify as "easy speed." This is training at the speed they are going to attain in competition but enough rest to sustain that speed and heart rate. A heart rate of 160 would be relatively "easy" and would be the maximum targeted heart rate for an "easy speed" set.

An example of an easy speed set would be 30 × 100 meters on a 2:00 send off and hold the 400 meter race pace for each 100. Your swimmers may need a longer recovery period to do this set and stay within the maximum heart rate. Swimmers learn to swim as fast as possible without straining to become accustomed to the feel of the physiological demands of 200 meters on up. Easy speed training should be considered in any training program.

The high school training season has most of the characteristics of the club model except that the season is much shorter. Three to four months is the maximum length of a high school season. It amounts to a compressed short-course season when compared with club swimming.

Sample Training Sessions

These workouts are taken from the team logbook and are based on the goals of the three training stages.

General endurance phase, week 7 of the short-course season:

1. Warm-up: 10 × 100, alternate free at 1:20, and individual medley (I.M.) at 1:30
2. Kick 12 × 100 at 1:40, descend 1 to 3
3. 4 (4 × 25 sprint at 0:40, and 2 × 50 sprint at 1:00) with parachutes
4. 5 × 400 pull with tube at 10 seconds rest
5. 12 × 200 free at 2:20 (subthreshold at two seconds over EN2 pace)
6. 24 × 25, I.M. order, stress technique
7. Cool-down: 10 × 50 at 0:45 (25 crawl, 25 back)

Specific endurance phase, week 15 of the short-course season:

1. Warm-up: 800 swim
2. 12 × 50 at 1:00, major stroke. Alternate (1) 12-1/2 sprint, 37-1/2 moderate, (2) 25 sprint, 25 moderate, (3) 37-1/2 sprint, 12-1/2 moderate, (4) 50 sprint.
3. 1 × 800 speed play, alternate 100 crawl of distance per stroke and 100 of major stroke build to a fast pace.
4. 20 × 50 pull with tube and paddles, odd number 25 crawl, 25 butterfly, even number 25 crawl, 25 breaststroke at five seconds rest
5. 12 × 50 at 0:50, odd number sprint, even number moderate crawl

Middle-distance/sprint group:

- 3 (3 × 200 free) at 2:20, EN2; 4 × 50 drill at 1:00, major stroke; 2 × 100 major stroke at 2:00, EN3
- 1 × 400 easy recovery swim
- 16 × 15-second sprint at 30 seconds rest on the stationary belts
- Cool-down: 400

Distance group:

- 8 × 400 free at 5:00, EN3
- 12 × 50 at 0:50, recovery (25 crawl, 25 butterfly drill)
- 15 × 100 at 1:15 (75 crawl, 25 butterfly)
- Cool-down: 400

Anaerobic and competition phase, week 21, short-course season:

1. Warm-up: 200 swim, 200 kick, 200 pull, 200 drills
2. 15 × 25 at 0:30 with paddles (15 yards sprint, 10 yards recovery)
3. 1 × 400 kick, alternate 50 moderate, 50 fast
4. 12 × 25 kick at 0:30, alternate moderate, strong build, and fast

5. 1 × 1200 pull, descend by 400s
6. 6 × 75 at 1:15 in major stroke (25 kick, 25 drill, 25 swim)
7. 5 × 100 at 1:40 (50 sprint in major stroke, 50 moderate crawl)

Middle-distance/sprint group:

- 12 × dive sprint 50 at 4:00, major stroke, 100 active rest recovery swim after each dive 50
- Cool-down: 5 × 100 at 1:40

Distance group:

- 3 × 400 at 4:40, descend 1 to 3 to EN2 pace
- 5 × 100 at 1:15, 1,650 race pace
- 3 × 300 at 3:30, descend 1 to 3 to EN2 pace
- 10 × 50 at 0:40, 1,000 race pace
- 3 × 200 at 2:20, descend 1 to 3 to EN2 pace
- 20 × 25 at 20, 500 race pace.
- Cool-down: 5 × 100 at 1:40

GENERAL ENDURANCE/HIGH SCHOOL SEASON

The main emphasis in the early season must be aerobic endurance training. Your endurance base is your foundation for sustained racing speed later in the season when you will need it most.

The intensity of training sets gradually increases in the early season. Training distances are longer and the rest intervals are short. I like to build into long kicking sets during the endurance buildup. Technique is emphasized, and the drills to be used throughout the season are taught at this time. Some speed work is done over short distances, up to 15 yards, during this training phase. Anaerobic threshold swimming can be introduced near the end of this period.

If the high school season is 15 weeks, only 3 weeks of these weeks could be set aside for general endurance. Ideally, this phase should start before the high school season begins and extend for a full 8 to 10 weeks. This is best done within club training but could be done by swimmers training on their own time.

SPECIFIC ENDURANCE/HIGH SCHOOL SEASON

Maximize the anaerobic threshold during this phase. In a 15-week high school season, you could assign about 5 weeks for specific endurance. Anaerobic training is seldom used during this phase but should be introduced into the final one and a half weeks with a minor emphasis only. Speed work over very short distances should be maintained. Correct technique and drills should be emphasized throughout this training. Adhere to the skills and drills that will be your model through the complete season.

This training period always coincided with winter holiday vacation in my high school coaching. We were able to overload the training volume for at least one week during this vacation period.

ANAEROBIC/HIGH SCHOOL

You could allow about four weeks of your high school season for this phase of training. Begin

Example of a High School Season Calendar

November 1—All required forms completed and turned in to the athletic director.

November 7—First day of swim practice.

November 24—Intrasquad meet and Thanksgiving vacation.

December 6—Dual meet.

December 9—Dual meet.

December 13—Dual meet.

December 16—Dual meet.

December 20—Dual meet.

December 23—Winter holiday vacation starts.

January 3—School resumes.

January 6—Dual meet.

January 13—Dual meet: a major city rival. (No rest but a special effort.)

January 16—Martin Luther King Jr. holiday.

January 20—Dual meet.

January 27—Dual meet.

February 4—District championship meet. (Taper, rest, and shave only for the non–state meet qualifiers.)

February 17, 18—State championship meet. (Taper, rest, and shave for all state meet participants.)

Training schedule:

December 1–23—Monday, Wednesday, and Friday training at 5:30 A.M.; Monday through Friday training at 2:45 P.M.; Saturday training at 8 A.M.

December 24–January 3—Monday through Saturday training at 8 A.M. and 2 P.M. (December 25 off, and morning session only on New Year's Day).

Special team meetings:

December 6—Our team approach to the dual meet season: uniform, team seating, teammate support, event selection, premeet warm-up, and postmeet training. December 12—Review the holiday training schedule and the goals for that training period. December 26—Motivational report from one or more of our returning college swimmers.

Special events:

December 2—Goals and split times due. December 24—Special training session. Week of December 26—one-on-one swimmer/coach conferences with all team members. Plan when and where your most intense training can best fit into this master calendar. Plan when and where the rest and the peak preparation will come.

to emphasize anaerobic training, speed 1 and 2. Maintain aerobic fitness but focus on speed and race pace. Specific race-pace training must be included at this time. You will maintain your swimmers' endurance through aerobic swimming but less frequently in this phase. EN2 sets are reduced slightly but still used about twice a week to maintain a good endurance base.

Continue the short sets of speed work over very short distances. Drills and technique work are maintained. Incorporate starts, turns, finishes, and relay exchanges during this period.

PEAK PREPARATION/ HIGH SCHOOL

This is your final phase of the high school season leading into the final championship meet. Speed training will reach its peak during this stage of the training season, but you should also continue some endurance training. Individualization of the training reaches a peak during this period.

It is time to sharpen your swimmers. Swimming at race pace should be precise and on target; everything must begin to come together. Peak preparation training is explained in chapter 13.

SPECIFICITY AND INDIVIDUALIZATION

Specific events require specific training for the best swimming results. The most successful programs are individualized to some degree to ensure the best results. Your team is made up of a variety of stroke specialists, sprinters, middle- to long-distance freestyle swimmers, and individual medley specialists. You will also have experienced and less experienced swimmers, seasonal and year-round swimmers, male and female swimmers, and swimmers of different ages. Each group has different needs.

Training must be specific to the needs of each swimmer at certain points in the training. Grouping swimmers for the most efficient and beneficial training session is a coaching

skill. Training must allow for differences, which means you may need to group your swimmers and plan the training session accordingly. Or, it may require only that you adjust the send-off times or the goal times for the individual team members.

After the general endurance phase of training, I always group swimmers into two or more groups. I have worked with as many as five groups, especially in the short high school swim season. This requires skilled planning and management. Your coaching organizational skills will be tested; however, the results will prove worth it.

The need for individualization and specificity in your training plan must be recognized. Coach Mike Bottom has carried specificity to an extreme for sprinters, and his successes are extraordinary. Gary Hall and Anthony Ervin tied for the gold medal in the Sydney Olympics in the 50-meter freestyle. Mike explains his freestyle sprint training in *The Swim Coaching Bible* (2001, Human Kinetics), and I recommend reading that chapter.

I ran a "super sprint" program for some high school swimmers when I coached high school swimming, yet I didn't do the same for my developing club swimmers. I wanted the year-round club swimmers to continue to develop their aerobic endurance base during those formative years.

GETTING READY PHYSICALLY

Preparing your swimmers is the key to a successful championship performance. Great personal fitness levels are essential for success. Examples of swimmers who attained elite fitness levels and then attained great swimming performances abound. Dara Torres swam in three Olympic Games and retired for almost seven years. She trained in a variety of physical activities, but not in swimming, over that time. At the age of 33, she made her fourth Olympic Team and earned medals at the best swimming times of her career. Dara and her coach Richard Quick agreed that Dara's superb fitness level made this possible.

My goal was to get our new high school swimmers into a very high level of physical fitness, and this continues throughout the year. All swimmers must reach and maintain great fitness levels in order to continue improving in the program; there is no going back or standing still in this matter.

The seasonal concept in high school sports promotes the idea that you can get into physical condition in the few weeks of the high school season. Nothing could be further from the truth. High school swimmers must be at an elevated level of personal physical fitness at the start of the swim season to be successful.

Progressive total fitness can make the difference between a good swimmer and a great one. Patient and continuous physical preparation is necessary. The "physical machine" that each swimmer brings to the starting blocks each year must be fitter and better than in the previous year. However, remember that this is a continuous and gradual process. Don't expect to make the difference in a short period of time.

Transition Training

Swimmers have a break at the end of the summer season, which may last up to four weeks. There will be another short break after the short-course winter season, usually during the school spring vacation. This swimming break should be short, one week or less. During these breaks in their training, swimmers can lose strength and endurance rapidly.

The best solution to maintain high fitness levels through breaks is cross-training, or what I call transition training. Swimming, in itself, won't prepare swimmers to be the best that they can be. Cross-training is necessary to maximize strength and to develop flexibility. My transition training minimizes swimming, although it would be best if the athlete continued to do some swimming at reduced distances. We even take a complete break from swimming for a very short time period to provide a better mental adjustment for the next serious swimming start.

However, I always continued our basics of 300 sit-ups and 100 push-ups each day. Aerobics, Pilates, yoga, jogging, running hills, biking, strength training, and even triathlons have all played a part in our transition training. Whatever you choose to incorporate into your program, try to provide something new in your swimmers' exercise program to spark their motivation.

Strength

I believe the core, particularly the abdominal area, of the body must be very strong. The ability of a swimmer to rotate quickly from side to side is most important. Our daily sit-ups contribute to this core strength, as does our use of medicine balls.

Strength in the extremities is also important and should be built through weight training, swim benches, swim sleds, medicine ball exercises, surgical tubing units, and specialty programs. Provide 30 to 60 minutes on most days for strength and flexibility training in addition to swimming. This is particularly true for the short-course season. Dry land strength equipment and sample dry land programs are discussed in chapter 13.

15-Week Plan for Typical High School Season

The main training emphasis for each session is your general guideline from which to build the training sets to be used in each daily session (see table 11.2).

Summary

1. Consider all ingredients necessary in your plan.
2. Build your plan around your master calendar.
3. Plan your training schedule for a full season or year.
4. Understand the terminology for the training systems.
5. Remember to communicate with swimmers and parents.
6. Emphasize physical fitness.
7. Train your swimmers to develop their core strength.
8. Make aerobic endurance the center of your training plan.
9. Individualize when needed for specificity.

Table 11.2   15-Week Training Plan

	Monday	Tuesday	Wednesday	Thursday	Friday	Saturday
Week 1						
A.M.	EN1	Off	EN1	OFF	EN1	EN1/SP3
P.M.	EN1	EN1/SP3	EN1+	EN1	EN1/SP3	Off
Week 2						
A.M.	EN1	Off	EN1	Off	EN1	EN2 Test
P.M.	EN1/SP3	EN1	EN1/SP3	EN1/SP3	EN1/SP3	Off
Week 3						
A.M.	EN1	Off	EN1	Off	EN1/SP3	EN2
P.M.	EN2	EN1/SP3	EN2/SP3	EN3	EN1/SP3	Off
Week 4						
A.M.	EN1/SP3	Off	EN1	Off	EN1/SP3	EN2/SP3
P.M.	EN2/SP3	EN3/SP3	EN1/SP3	EN2/SP3	EN1/SP3	OFF
Week 5						
A.M.	EN1/SP3	OFF	EN1/SP3	OFF	EN1	EN2/SP3
P.M.	EN2	EN3/SP3	EN1/SP3	EN2/SP3	SP1/SP3	Off
Week 6						
A.M.	EN1/SP3	Off	EN1	Off	EN2	EN2Test
P.M.	EN1	EN2/SP3	EN1/SP3	EN3	EN1/SP3	Off
Week 7						
A.M.	EN1/SP3	Off	EN1	Off	EN1	EN2/SP3
P.M.	EN2	EN1/SP3	EN3/SP3	EN1/SP3	EN1	Off
Week 8						
A.M.	EN1/SP3	Off	EN1	Off	EN1/SP3	EN3/SP3
P.M.	EN2	EN1/SP3	EN3/SP3	EN1/SP1	EN1	Off
Week 9						
A.M.	EN1/SP3	Off	EN1	Off	EN1/SP3	EN2/SP3
P.M.	SP1/EN1	EN2/SP3	EN3/SP3	EN1	SP2/EN1	Off
Week 10						
A.M.	EN1	Off	EN1/SP3	Off	EN1/SP3	EN2/SP3
P.M.	EN3/SP3	SP2/SP3	EN2/EN1	EN1/SP3	SP1/EN1	Off
Week 11						
A.M.	EN1	Off	EN1/SP3	Off	EN1/SP3	SP2/SP3
P.M.	SP2/SP3	EN2/EN1	EN1/SP3	SP1/EN1	EN2	Off
Week 12						
A.M.	EN1	Off	EN1	Off	EN1/SP3	EN2/SP3
P.M.	SP2/SP3	EN2/SP3	SP1/SP3	EN3/SP3	SP2/EN1	Off
Weeks 13-15 (Peak preparation or taper period—see chapter 13.)						

Chapter 12

PREPARING FOR PRACTICES

After you plan your season, it is almost time to begin practice. Before swimmers take their first strokes, you need to prepare for the practice sessions by making plans that detail what training equipment is necessary and how best to use it, how to enhance the pool environment effectively, how to assign lanes in an effective manner, and other assorted but important details that make your practice sessions successful.

THE ESSENTIALS

Each prospective swimmer must fulfill a number of preliminary requirements to join the swim team. The high school swimmer usually must provide the following:

1. Results of a medical screening
2. Proof of insurance
3. Evidence of student activity membership
4. A completed parental permission form

The high school athletic director will often assume the responsibility of making sure your swimmers meet these requirements. Make certain that your athletes meet their responsibilities before the first scheduled practice.

Our Tacoma Swim Club registration chairperson assumes this responsibility for my club swimmers. Each family must complete a medical form, register in USA Swimming, and become a club member in order to be a participant. Although I like to make certain each swimmer completes this process, I prefer to have someone else specialize in carrying out this procedure.

FACILITIES AND POOL SETUP

Although you will not be able to make many changes in the structure of your training pool, you can change the pool environment to make it conducive to competitiveness.

We did have one exception to changing pool structure. Tacoma Swim Club actually changed the length of our city outdoor pool. Originally it was a 55-yard pool and remained that way for 39 years. Our club changed the length to 50 meters. An additional concrete wall of about 12 inches was added to the shallow end of the pool to make this possible. All of the materials were donated, and our club members volunteered the labor. We now have a regulation 50-meter course pool.

Maintain the water of your pool at the correct level to minimize surface water turbulence. Lane lines that are the best for turbulence control are also a necessity, and they must be able to be installed rapidly.

You will need a great deal of other equipment to begin your practices. Backstroke flags must be in place at every training session, so your backstroke swimmers and individual medley swimmers can practice all of their turns effectively and legally. Starting blocks should be in place for organized and supervised starts. Pace clocks must be in place and visible from every lane at both ends of the pool. Bulletin boards, white boards, and chalkboards must also be available for announcements and posting the day's training session for your swimmers.

I always had special interest display boards at Wilson High School, with one section containing a list of All American swimmers from our school and another listing all of the Wilson High School state individual and relay event champions. I also had a special section for every high school team that won a state championship. Our team records board was a large 4 × 8 foot board with large letters to print the names of our swimmers who held records.

A very special section to our swimmers was the honor roll boards. Each swimming event had a special kickboard attached to the wall of the pool. In order to have their names placed on the honor roll board, the swimmers had to attain a very fast and specified time for that event.

Finally, we had two super boards placed above the honor roll boards. One board was for those athletes who attained the honor roll time in every event, and the other was for those who broke a national high school record.

Additional Needs

Student managers are a great help in making your practice sessions very efficient. I have always had several of the brightest young students available to assist me each day of my high school program.

The ability to time every swimmer whenever the need arises in practice is only possible when you have enough capable student managers. The records boards, the daily motivational point tables, and the bulletin board are all areas of responsibility for your student managers.

In swim meets, your student managers can take the split times and can keep the running score during the competitions. They can also handle many other responsibilities that may range from the placement of special equipment in the pool area for the competition to getting the meet results to the newspapers, radio, and television outlets.

Medical Precautions

During practice and competitions, Wilson High School had a trainer on duty in the gym and in the pool buildings. Swim coaches must have CPR and first aid training at minimum. USA Swimming club coaches must have Coaches' Safety Training. Whatever emergency training is required, the emphasis remains on accident prevention. A contingency plan to respond to a pool accident must be in place and should be reviewed and rehearsed each season. Post the emergency number at the nearest telephone along with the instructions that need to be relayed.

Nutritional Guidelines

"Invisible training," those habits of preparation that are hidden from the coach, refers to the nutrition, the amount of sleep, and the rest that a swimmer attains. Good invisible training is vital for the success of your swim teams. Your swimmers can't recover quickly from one practice session to another without adequate sleep, rest, and nutrition.

One of our young high school swimmers was at a plateau, discouraged because he was training hard and swimming slower. I asked him when he usually went to bed. He said he was retiring somewhere between 11 P.M. and midnight and then getting up at 5 A.M. He believed that this was the only way he could maintain his academic goals. I suggested that he organize his available study time and get to bed by 9:30 P.M. He agreed reluctantly, but within two weeks, he attained best ever swims in his events. His training also improved dramatically and, to his relief, his academic achievements didn't suffer. He was already an honor student and continued so.

During school vacations, I encourage daily naps between the two training sessions. Most of our swimmers have learned to take advantage of this invisible training necessity.

ROSTER AND EVENTS

I accept every swimmer who can swim safely and has some technical proficiency in the competitive swimming strokes. Likewise, you shouldn't worry about accepting too many athletes. A few will always drop out when they realize the degree of discipline, time, and effort that is involved to be successful. You don't know which swimmers will commit to the program until you give them the opportunity.

Swimmers can always be assigned to events as your team needs become clear. I coach all of my swimmers as individual medley swimmers in their early training, because it stresses all four strokes in my teaching and training. If you use this individual medley training attitude, you will produce your specialists in time. Swimmers will also have the ability to fill in for any event when the need arises.

Setting Up the Practice Schedule

I usually scheduled two training sessions per day on Mondays, Wednesdays, and Fridays during the school year and every day but Wednesdays and Saturdays during summer vacation. We trained at least once a day, except on Sundays.

Because swimming is easier on the muscles and the joints than other sports (e.g., running), there is less risk of injuries. Consequently, you can do double workouts within each week when practical during the school year, with the exception of maybe early season and peak preparation periods. Also remember that stress levels are always higher when school is in session, so increased practice sessions are possible during the summer and vacation periods.

Length of Practice

During the school year, we train one and a half hours before school on the days of our morning workouts. Our afternoon sessions are usually two and a half to three hours, including the meetings and dry land training. Normally I schedule a three and a half hour practice on Saturday mornings. I make an exception to this in May and June when preparing for the long-course season and add a second workout on Saturday afternoons for the last month of school to better prepare our swimmers for summer training sessions.

I schedule a three-hour practice session each morning during the summer, including the dry land training and meetings. I then schedule a two-hour practice session in the afternoons, except for Wednesdays and Saturdays, which are off. Sundays are not scheduled training days throughout the year. You may have to alter your schedule according to the availability of the swimming pool.

What is the ideal length of a practice session? Most teams have less time available than I have outlined in this chapter. This should never be the reason not to pursue swimming success. Just use the pool space and the available time that you do have. Regardless of limitations, you can always be successful when you take full advantage of your situation. Swimmers have succeeded at even the Olympic level on much less time and pool space than I have indicated to be ideal.

> **Regardless of limitations, you can always be successful when you take full advantage of your situation.**

THE TRAINING COURSE

Utilize the course that you have. I never had long course available during the school year, except on rare occasions. We trained primarily short course during the school year in 25-yard or 25-meter pools. When a long-course pool was available during winter vacation or spring break, we took advantage of that opportunity. Long-course training accelerates endurance training, but it is not often available. If you don't have a long-course pool available when preparing for long-course competition, increase your yardage totals and add to the distance of your repeat swims. For example, do 10 × 225 or 250, instead of 10 × 200.

During the long-course summer season, we train in a 50-meter pool six mornings each week. I schedule our afternoon workouts in a short-course pool a couple times each week, because I believe that swimmers will maintain more speed and a faster stroking tempo in short-course training.

Another option we have in our short-course pools is the cross-pool course. During both the long- and short-course seasons, I train cross-pool when available to emphasize and maintain speed. My cross-pool course is over a 35- or 45-foot course depending on the pool we are using. Swimmers do more turns in cross-pool training, and they can swim at very fast speeds with less effort because of the speed attained pushing off the walls. Training cross-pool is also good for quality control, because you can communicate technique tips more frequently with the swimmer always close at hand.

ASSIGNING LANES

The wall lanes, unless they are extra wide, should not be used by backstroke, butterfly, or breaststroke swimmers, because they need enough lane space to maintain good technique. Your swimmers can't learn their strokes if they are hitting or trying to avoid hitting the wall while swimming. Crawl stroke will not have this problem.

In a six-lane pool with narrow wall lanes, assign one wall lane for the sprint freestyle swimmers. Sprint freestyle swimmers are less of a distraction to other swimmers at one side of the pool, because they rest more in their sets. They also move to our diving well for cross-pool swimming and to the swim benches more often within the practice.

For similar reasons, place your breaststroke swimmers next to the sprint lane. Then you can use two lanes for the backstroke and butterfly swimmers, which will allow you to give them the same send-off time. Such an arrangement will leave two lanes for the middle-distance and distance crawl swimmers.

This particular example would place swimmers in the lanes as follows:

Lane 1: sprint crawl

Lane 2: breaststroke

Lane 3: backstroke can be combined with butterfly

Lane 4: butterfly can be combined with backstroke

Lanes 5 and 6: middle-distance and distance crawl

Individual medley swimmers would be placed in appropriate lanes for each day's stroke specialization. If you have more or less than six lanes, you can adjust your options accordingly.

Circle Patterns

I prefer placing lane lines in between every two lanes instead of every one. Using a line between every other lane saves us time in setting up the pool for practice and again at the end. The swimmers circle clockwise in the odd-numbered lanes and counterclockwise in the even-numbered lanes (see figure 12.1). This permits better opportunities to pass by crossing to another lane when necessary, and it also reduces the risk of collisions.

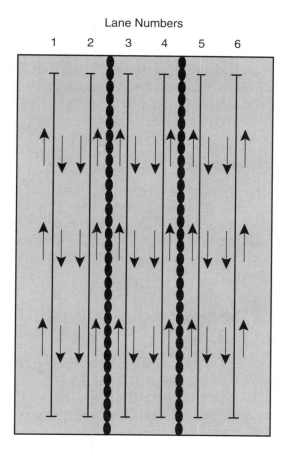

Figure 12.1   Lane circle patterns.

TRAINING AIDS

I believe that to attain maximum success from your swimmers, you need a variety of effective training aids. Aids can enhance the teaching of stroke technique and maximize the training effect. The use of training aids breaks up the routine for the swimmers, which is another advantage as well.

I recommend using a number of swimming aids wherever they enhance your program. Some are more vital than others, and I will make that distinction. I have experimented with many training aids; I made hand paddles, underwater mirrors, and drag materials before they ever became commercially available.

Hand Paddles

I have long believed that paddles should be an aid for teaching above any other consideration. I designed my first paddles to enhance the swimmers' feel of the water and to increase their distance per stroke. When solid plastic paddles became available, I used them for many years, but I wasn't satisfied with their ability to improve stroke technique.

Consequently, I designed a unique hand paddle that had holes over the complete paddle. The black Han's Paddle was the first holed paddle. The holes allowed water to flow through the paddle, which enhanced the feel of water on the hand. The holes also allow a faster stroking tempo than solid plastic paddles and present less risk of joint and muscle injury.

Subsequently I designed two more holed paddles with a grooved tread on the water side. The two were progressively oversized paddles, named Groover and Gripper. All of the paddles were designed for use in all four strokes.

Han's Paddle is a regular-sized paddle designed to improve technique and power. The Gripper is a technique paddle that maximizes the distance per stroke. The Groover is larger than the Han's Paddle and smaller than the Gripper. Swimmers learn how to move their body forward past the stroking arm when using any swim paddle.

Swim Fins

Use a short swim fin for power kicking. The shorter fin requires a faster and more intensive kick from the swimmer, with a range almost the same as in speed swimming. The short fin builds power in the legs. You can either cut the regular size fins shorter or you can purchase short fins. I suggest a softer shoe on the fin, because it is less irritating to the feet.

Fins continue to be improved. There are now fins that are effective for use in the breaststroke kick as well as the flutter and dolphin kicks.

Rubber Bands

All of my swimmers had their own large rubber band to wear around their ankles when pulling. Rubber bands are good in all strokes, especially the backstroke.

Goggles

Swim goggles are a must in training at every age level. I can't believe that we used to train for hours without them. Goggles help your swimmers see better when judging the walls at turns, but mainly they help them avoid eye irritation from pool chemicals.

Tethered Swim Belts and Tubing

I use tethered swim belts and surgical tubing for tethered swimming. The long belts are tethered at the end of the pool. Stationary belts are tethered on the lane lines at both sides of the swimmer. Stationary belts permit a number of swimmers to train on belts within one lane.

The short tubing with an attached belt need only be 6 to 12 feet in length to permit power kicking, pulling, or swimming to a tension point. Longer tubing will permit both tethered swimming for the pool's full length and a speed-assisted return to the starting point. In speed-assisted swimming, a second person on the pool deck pulls the tubing, helping the swimmer attain very fast speeds to the wall. There are also power reels that mechanically do the same thing but are much more expensive.

Mirrors

I have used a wall mirror during most of my coaching career. The mirror serves as a technique coach for backstroke swimmers. At deck level, place a body-length mirror at the end wall of your pool. Angle the top of the mirror away from the wall so your swimmers can watch themselves swimming backstroke as they move away from the mirror. The mirror is also effective for standing drills facing the mirror in the other strokes.

Water Bottles

Each swimmer must have his or her own water bottle for personal use throughout the training session. Water or a special training drink is each swimmer's choice.

Kickboards

I prefer that most kicking be done without kickboards. However, some kicking should be done on a kickboard. These are usually done in the fast intensive sets. A smaller kickboard works best so that buoyancy isn't over-emphasized.

Pull Buoys and Inner Tubes

Pull buoys help streamline the lower body and hold it high enough in the water to simulate the position swimmers will have when moving fast. Use the smaller or medium-sized pull buoys for best results. Larger pull buoys lift most swimmers too high in the water and make training too easy. I don't believe that backstroke swimmers should use pull buoys. I prefer the band with no buoyancy support in backstroke.

We used inner tubes in our program to provide swimmers with added resistance when pulling. I prefer the four-inch diameter inner tubes. Inner tubes can be used effectively with pull buoys to increase resistance while still retaining some of the advantages of the pull buoy buoyancy.

Parachutes and Buckets

Swimming and pulling with a parachute or a bucket attached to the swimmer provide additional increased resistance

Power Racks

Power racks are good for measuring and developing power in the water. You can measure your swimmers' improvement by the weight they can pull and the time they take to do a short swim. Sprinters love to work on the power rack, especially when you challenge them by timing their swim and increasing their resisting weight. It is an expensive piece of equipment but worthy of a fund-raising project.

Miscellaneous Aids

Many other aids should be used to evaluate your swimmers' effectiveness. Drag suits increase resistance while swimming. For some special training, I use soft divers' weight belts. Swimming with tennis shoes, shirts, or pants adds water resistance. A word of caution: Using any equipment that places the body in an incorrect position can be detrimental; you should evaluate the beneficial potential of any new equipment.

DRY LAND TRAINING

Supplement your swimmers' strength and power training with dry land training. Schedule a designated time for your dry land training when the equipment and facilities are available. Your time training out of the pool will also change during the course of the swim season according to the phase of your in-pool training. During the peak preparation period, your dry land training will decrease considerably, and it will be at its highest point during transition training.

My dry land program changed every season according to my team's training phases and the availability of equipment and facilities. My dry land program includes the following: surgical tubing units, swim benches and swim sleds, medicine ball training, basic exercises, flexibility exercises, and weight training. However, I couldn't possibly use all of these on any one day because of time constraints and equipment availability. I suggest rotating specific groups of swimmers through your planned dry land training on alternate days. Such an arrangement will result in maximum use of the equipment you have available.

Surgical Tubing Units

Surgical tubing units are inexpensive and can be safely anchored to diving board railings and to wall eyebolts. I like to have them anchored at a position above shoulder height. Your swimmers, at minimal risk of injury to themselves, can duplicate swimming movements closely, resulting in an increased power and endurance that will transfer effectively to their swimming.

I use these units every season, and each swimmer owns his or her own. I prefer a paddle at each end of the tubing to simulate the hand position while swimming.

Here is a sample training session using a surgical tubing unit:

Perform each exercise for 30 repeats or one minute. Do the repeats of each exercise with fast movement but perfect technique. Perform three sets of each exercise in numerical order:

1. Butterfly full stroke
2. Elbow forward extension presses
3. Lateral forward arm swings
4. Butterfly recovery
5. Butterfly finish
6. Butterfly full stroke (a second set)
7. Backstroke pull-downs
8. Breaststroke pull

One round of this particular set would take 24 minutes. The number of repeats and the rest interval would depend on the stage of the season. This particular set would probably be used in midseason. Emphasize that each set must be done with perfect technique and fast execution.

Swim Benches or Swim Sleds

Swim benches and swim sleds are both units on which the swimmers lie in a prone position and simulate a swimming stroke, usually butterfly. On the swim bench the body remains stationary, and the machine setting determines the amount of resistance that the arm stroke will have to overcome. Swim benches can usually give you a power rating that is scored electronically.

On the swim sled, swimmers lie on a movable platform and pull their body past their arms, as they do in actual swimming. The swim bench helps the athlete attain the feeling of swimming while providing additional resistance. The body doesn't move past the arms on the bench, but your swimmers can duplicate fast swimming strokes with variable resistance.

Pair up your swimmers, with one doing the bench or sled exercises and the partner performing sit-ups, push-ups, or some other exercise while waiting. A typical sled set would be 5 × 20 repeats with good technique and a power pull on the sled. Partners would alternate on the sled after each set of 20. The swim bench set would vary the resistance and the number of repeats according to the stroke and distance swum.

Medicine Balls

Medicine ball training increases core strength as well as strength of the extremities. Review a list of recommended medicine ball exercises to determine which best serve your needs.

In using medicine balls, I like twist and turn drills, passing drills, and stomach exercises. You can create many interesting and motivational drills with medicine balls.

Basic Exercises

Our basic daily exercises include a minimum of 300 sit-ups and 100 push-ups. When I have suitable equipment, I add pull-ups and dips to our program. The sit-ups and push-ups take very little time and can be done anywhere that is convenient to the swimmer.

Provide your swimmers with some time for flexibility exercises before they go into the water. At the Australian Institute of Sport, where a specialist teaches flexibility exercises at the start of each session, the swimmers report to practice 15 minutes early to do their exercises.

You must sell your swimmers on the benefits of being flexible. Teach them the necessary exercises at the start of the season. There are a number of excellent sources for flexibility exercises, including a booklet published by USA Swimming. (One Olympic Plaza, Colorado Springs, CO 80909-5770)

Weight training has been an area of controversy for swimmers, because it is a form of dry land training that can increase the risk of injury and can bulk up a streamlined body. However, it can also help to prevent injuries when supervised and done properly. You need to research and understand the effects of weight training before introducing it into a program. The American Swim Coaches Association has an excellent study course on dry land training.

I believe in weight training for some swimmers, because most swimmers will develop more strength and speed as a result of it. On the other hand, many great distance coaches do not believe in any weight training because they want to avoid any additional bulk and other possible negative results from the use of weights. I suggest that distance swimmers be more cautious in their approach to weight training. You should approach weight training based on individual needs and abilities.

Age-group swimmers who have not gone through puberty should use gymnastics and any other dry land opportunities that meet the requirements of their physical maturity. I didn't use weight training for my age-group swimmers, but if you decide to do so, base your decision on the best research available on the subject.

When I had a weight-training room available in my high school, I used it for my boys' team three times a week for about 45 minutes each session. Because I don't have a weight-training room available as a club coach, I use the other forms of dry land training.

MAKING PRACTICES EFFECTIVE AND FUN

If you can make each practice effective and fun, without any conflict, then you have mastered the art of coaching. The greatest fun for swimmers is to swim fast at the season's end in their championship meet. I remind my swimmers of this fact whenever necessary to keep them focused on their goals. However, it is also true that all work and no play makes for dull swimmers.

Every workout must have a purpose in order to be effective. Whenever practical, explain the training plan before practice. Our swimmers commit to practice with more enthusiasm when they understand the goals of the training plan.

I have used the following methods in practice to provide my swimmers with some light moments and opportunities to relax, while at the same time keeping focused on their goals.

Starting Practice

Getting swimmers into the water can be a big hurdle each day. I've tried a lot of things from threats to physical assists. Whatever your methods, you'll find that the things that work best are fun for all.

I like the "backstroke flag goggle lag." Swimmers get one chance at the start of practice to throw their goggles onto the backstroke flag line. If their goggles land and hold on the line, they win a power bar from me. Everyone then gets into the water to retrieve their goggles, and practice starts.

I used another fun gimmick to start practice in our outdoor summer pool, where each swimmer got to throw one kickboard from the starting end down the pool. We determined our male and female division winners according to the distance that the kickboard traveled.

Remember, however, that this gimmick requires close supervision to keep all swimmers behind the throwing line until all tosses are completed; otherwise, it could be a safety risk.

Getting Too Good

The kickboard throw was very popular on my team for several years, but when the young men on one particular team began to throw the kickboards over the fence beyond the length of our 50-meter pool, I had to review the contest. I could marshal the pool area but I couldn't control the people and the automobiles in the parking lot, so it was time to change the game.

Right On Cards

We use Tacoma Swim Club Right On Cards in training. Whenever a swimmer catches a teammate doing something right, the swimmer makes a mental note of it. After practice, the swimmer completes a Right On Card, stating exactly what that teammate did correctly. Finally, the swimmer dates, signs, and gives the card to the teammate.

We have had contests each week where the swimmer who gives and receives the most cards gets a prize. Swimmers can only win if they are both giving and receiving cards. This helps all our swimmers stay positive.

Special Workouts

Designing a workout by chance, listing training sets and selecting them randomly, is fun for the swimmers. Dart throwing, rolling dice, and drawing cards are good ways to determine training sets.

I conducted a special Christmas Eve workout each year, where swimmers had fun by chancing their way to a "Scrooge" set or a "little elves at play" set. If the swimmers chance their way to a Scrooge, they get hit with an intensive swimming set, but when their chance comes up little elves at play, they get a playful set.

My favorite little elves at play sets include surf's up, three on two kickboards, whirlpool, stacking kickboards, and tow your buddy. Explanations of each follow. Winners always receive prizes, such as a power bar, fruit, or even a candy cane.

Surf's Up

Have your swimmers stand on the pool bottom and form two lines along two swimming lanes, extending the lines most of the pool's length. Leave one lane open without lines, for a swimmer.

Then, have the swimmers use their kickboards to create as many waves as possible. Select a swimmer to time trial a 50-yard butterfly between the two lines of swimmers and through the surf.

Whirlpool

Form your swimmers in a large circle in the shallow end; have them walk and then run in a circle, first clockwise and then counterclockwise. Reversing direction is always a major challenge. After a time, get the circle going as fast as possible in one direction, forming a giant whirlpool. Have your swimmers move into the maximum flow and sprint the length of the pool.

Three on Two Kickboards

Three swimmers overlap on two kickboards, and they race other such teams through a process of elimination to determine a champion. The middle swimmer of the three holds each of the two kickboards by one arm. The swimmer on the left holds onto the left kickboard with his or her left arm and reaches over the middle swimmer's arm to hold the right kickboard with his or her right arm. This position is reversed for the swimmer on the right. All three swimmers are shoulder to shoulder on two kickboards.

Stacking Kickboards

In the deep end of the pool, have a swimmer try with both feet to sink a floating kickboard without falling off. Each time a swimmer is eliminated, add one kickboard for those remaining. Subsequent rounds will have two, three, four, and then five or more kickboards until one swimmer is declared champion. The elimination process occurs with a limited number of swimmers going at the same time.

Tow Your Buddy

One swimmer holds the ankle of the leader and is towed for 25 yards, and then the swimmers reverse for the second 25 yards. Teams race off until a winner is declared.

SPECIAL CONSIDERATIONS

When do fun items become necessary for your team? When you aren't having fun and aren't excited in the training sessions, you can be certain that your swimmers need a lift too. Change can provide a lift and put a smile on some faces.

You can incorporate a great number of fun items into almost any workout. Relays are always fun; try them with such crazy strokes as the corkscrew stroke and the butterfly with a flutter kick.

Unexpected change is fun. Try having your swimmers run in the pool for part of their repeats. Have them swim a 30×50 with the first and last 12-1/2 yards running instead of swimming. Not only does this provide variety for your swimmers, it also gets their heart rates up for an intense workout.

You can also try handicap relays, where you stagger your swimmers' starts in order to make them play catch-up or hold-off depending on their positions.

The single file and sprint drill was one of my favorites in the long-course pool. Athletes would swim in a tight single file, and the last one would sprint to the front of the line. When that swimmer took the lead, he or she would slow the pace again, and the new last swimmer would sprint to the front of the line.

Circuit training—moving from one section of the pool to another to complete a circuit—can be a challenging and entertaining change from the usual routine.

How often you insert fun items into your training will depend on the age of your swimmers and your enthusiasm and creativity. If you use special workouts too often, you can lose your focus, and your swimmers can lose interest.

Some fun sessions are best done after practice if time permits. One of my high school teams played a short game of water volleyball after each practice, organizing into teams by class level. The backstroke flags served as net, and I was the referee. Although our backstroke flags were tattered and torn, our team bond was stronger for playing water volleyball.

One of the best methods I used as a high school coach to maintain focus and have fun doing it involved keeping a season-long point chart. All members of the Wilson High School swim team were listed on that chart and started the season with about 50 minus points; they had to dig their way out of a hole from the very start of the season.

I gave them minus points for everything I could think of: average grades, no long-course summer season, a family member who was formerly on the team, long hair, good looks, shyness, or whatever. It used to be a matter of pride when a swimmer ended up with the most minus points, giving him or her bragging rights and creating a few laughs.

Swimmers could earn plus points by displaying great training habits or by personal best times for kicking, pulling, or swimming sets in practice. Personal best meet times and attaining qualifying time standards for state, sectionals, Junior Nationals when held, and Senior Nationals also earned points. Outside of practice and competition, good grades and attendance in school would get them some plus points.

A certain number of points earned a popcorn ball, a milkshake, or an ice cream sundae. On the other hand, a swimmer who ended up with minus points might end up washing my car or cleaning up in my home.

We had a party at my home about two weeks before the championship meet, and I paid off the popcorn balls and other prizes to the swimmers. We also used this party to watch meet films of our previous success in state meets and to talk about the coming championship.

SUMMARY

Preparing for practices takes time and creativity from the coach. The following elements can help you better prepare for your training sessions with your swimmers:

1. Make up a written practice schedule, which will depend on available pool time.
2. Assign lanes by stroke and distance.
3. Use circle patterns, alternating them by lanes.
4. Be sure that the necessary competitive meet equipment is in place for practice.
5. Use some swimming aids for maximum individual success.
6. Make practice fun while maintaining the focus on goals.
7. Supplement your water training with dry land training.
8. Preplan to ensure that your swimmers complete the necessary paperwork.
9. Remember that student managers are a necessity for a good program.
10. Stress to your swimmers the importance of invisible training—proper amounts of sleep, rest, and nutrition.
11. Begin your swimmers in individual medley training, which will fill the gaps in the events.

Part IV

COACHING MEETS

Chapter
13

PREPARING FOR MEETS

It's important to vary the type of preparation for swim meets, because all meets aren't equally important. You have already used your master calendar to determine which meets have the highest priority. Your championship meet is the major one on which to maintain your focus.

READYING YOUR TEAM

Train your swimmers, providing them consistent stress levels throughout each week of the season according to your plan. Do the sets scheduled for that day's master plan at the intensity level necessary to meet the objectives of the training categories explained in chapter 11. The championship meet is your goal meet. All other meets must help prepare your swimmers to do their best at the championship. Athletes must not become too dependent on their coach for strategies, ideas, and evaluation. The more independent athletes become as they mature, the tougher they are in pressure situations.

Swimming is not like football, basketball, or many other team sports. In most sports, every game is important in order to make the playoffs or to win the league championship. Consequently, coaches of these sports cannot risk having their athletes too exhausted to compete at their best in the league competition.

On the other hand, the championship in swimming is usually decided at the championship meet. The team that scores the most points at that one competition wins. As a result, you need to train your athletes through most of the league meets to effectively taper and rest them for the final championship competition.

Too Much Too Soon!

Some high school and club teams swim fast in all or most of their regular season meets and then fail at their championship. Every year that I have coached, I've seen this from some teams. I learned quickly that swimmers must have a consistent training program throughout the season that is focused on the championship meet. This was the only way that I could get high-level performances from my swimmers when we swam at the championship meet.

This doesn't mean that fast swimming during the season is detrimental in itself. Fast swimming is a confidence builder and an indication of each swimmer's potential. Just don't sacrifice the training plan by attempting to taper or peak for every competition. Maintain your aerobic endurance training, and possibly increase some fast swimming going into a couple of in-season meets. Make this a part of your season plan and let the competitions be your anaerobic training days. This often works well in the longer club season and when you have fewer meets.

High school swimming is too short and has too many meets to adjust the training load for meets. I preferred to train through every meet possible, if not all the meets. My high school team wasn't always seeded first going into the state championship meet. The top swimming times that are recorded during the regular dual meet season determine the rankings and the favorite team going into the championship meet. Our regular season swimming times may not have been the best, but our state championship times were always at the top.

Too many coaches rest their teams too often during the season. Keep your ego under control and have confidence in your training calendar. I've seen too many coaches who wanted fast times from their swimmers too soon in the season. Be patient and take some risks in the regular season schedule, even if it means an unwelcome loss. The key is to be there when it counts most.

Types of Meets

Dual meets make up most of the schedule in high school and college swimming and are also used in club and YMCA swimming but less often. In club swimming, invitational meets make up most of the schedule, but they are also used in YMCA, high school, and college swimming. Invitational meets include many teams and can take very long to complete.

Preparing for Regular Season Meets

Prepare for the regular season meets as though they were another training session. I agree with the expression, "Competition is the purest form of training." You can never duplicate racing conditions in training as you do in actual competition. You should consider competitive races as speed training for swimmers and as an opportunity to test them in competition.

Plan a long warm-up and cool-down before and after the competition. The fans, officials, and rival teams will enhance the competitive atmosphere and will ensure that swimmers make a good effort.

What makes a regular season meet more important? Competing against a traditional team rival or needing to swim fast enough to meet the qualifying standards for the championship meet would be two good reasons. Sometimes an invitational meet will attract high-quality competition to make it somewhat special.

One example of a special meet in our club schedule was The Canada Cup meet, in Vancouver, British Columbia. Some of the best swimmers in the world attended this meet, including teams from Australia, China, Sweden, Italy, and the United States. Although we traveled just 185 miles to compete in the Canada

Cup, the fact that it occurred in a foreign country gave the meet an added significance.

Giving swimmers one or two mornings off from training during the week of a special meet is acceptable. Swimmers should avoid intense anaerobic training for a few days prior to the meet, and they should maintain general aerobic endurance, speed, and stroke technique. Most of the swimming should be aerobic, which should help each swimmer race well in the competition without losing any training effect.

Preparing for the championship meet is a whole other story. Your swimmers have directed their entire season toward success at this meet. Follow your season training plan up to the time period that you have designated for peak preparation, a process some coaches call "tapering."

I prefer to call it peak preparation, because it minimizes the taper mentality that emphasizes only rest. Prepare swimmers for some very specific training at this time, focusing on every technical aspect, the most important ones being starts, turns, finishes, optimum distance per stroke, stroke tempo, and race strategies.

One of the arts in coaching is the delicate balance between tapering and full training. Tapering too long can produce great speed but can leave the swimmer unable to sustain that speed over the complete race. Conversely, tapering for too short a time can leave swimmers flat and without the speed they need to be successful.

THE PEAK PREPARATION PERIOD

Some believe that the most important aspect of coaching is determining the length and intensity of the taper for each swimmer. Your self-confidence and your swimmers' confidence in your taper are vital for success. The peak preparation period should be long enough to permit the flexibility needed to adjust the taper's length and the intensity of its swimming.

As a coach of male swimmers, I planned my high school season peak preparation to last about three weeks. Some swimmers needed more time, and some needed less. The high school championship meet is a short meet with fewer events than a club championship meet. For those reasons, a longer taper was generally more successful than a short peak preparation period. A few swimmers always tapered longer than others, so I adjusted for each individual from a general plan of three weeks.

Consider all of the following factors before you decide on the length of your peak preparation, because these will affect the length planned for each swimmer. Remember that you need flexibility to meet the swimmer's individual needs:

1. Whether the swimmer is male or female
2. Whether the swimmer is a sprinter or distance swimmer
3. The swimmer's muscle mass
4. The length and type of championship meet
5. The swimmer's history
6. Whether the event is a short-course or long-course championship
7. The apparent effect of the season's training
8. The swimmer's age

Male or Female

The taper for male swimmers must be longer than for female swimmers in most situations, because men take longer to recover from intense training. If my peak preparation is going to be over a three-week period for male swimmers, then I would shorten this to two weeks for most female swimmers.

Sprint or Distance Swimmer

Sprint swimmers taper over a longer period than middle-distance and distance swimmers.

For your distance swimmers, maintain intensive training and adequate aerobic endurance training closer to the championship meet. I normally shorten the taper period for distance swimmers by at least one week or more compared with sprinters.

The middle-distance swimmers, those who compete primarily at the 200 and 400/500 events, would fall between the sprint and distance swimmers in the length of the peak preparation.

Swimmer's Muscle Mass

Men generally need a longer taper than women, because of their muscle mass. This is also true within each sex; heavily muscled men usually need to taper more than those with less muscle density, and the more densely muscled women will usually need more rest or a longer taper than those with less density.

Length and Type of Championship Meet

A high school state championship meet is normally a one- or two-day meet. When it is two days, the prelims are usually one day and the finals the next. A USA Swimming National Championship meet is over four days or longer, and the Olympic trials are sometimes as long as eight days. Preparing for a short one- to two-day meet permits a longer peak preparation period than would be used for a longer meet.

History of the Swimmer

Know your swimmers and keep records of what works best for each individual. I have had swimmers who tapered best over a very long peak preparation period of about five weeks. These are usually heavily muscled male swimmers in the short-course season, and their primary events are the 50 freestyle or any of the stroke 100s.

I have also had swimmers that needed to train very close to the meet, a few days, up to 10 days. Normally, I would consider a 10-day taper to be on the short end of a short-course peak preparation period. In the long-course season, 10-day tapers have worked well with my male distance swimmers and most of my

females. Some female swimmers find 7-day tapers successful for the long-course season.

Anything shorter than seven days is cutting it close, but it may be necessary for swimmers who are low in self-confidence. Although you really need to taper these swimmers longer, you also need to build their confidence by giving them enough easy swimming that they believe that they are still working.

Short Course or Long Course

Long-course events are longer distance than the equivalent short-course events. The 100 meters is almost 10 yards longer than a 100-yard event.

The difference in swimming a 100-meter event in long course is not just the additional distance compared with a 100-yard race but also the fact that a long-course 100 event requires only one turn, whereas the short-course 100 yards requires three turns. This means that the athlete is not swimming when he or she turns and pushes off the wall. The difference between a long-course 100 and a short-course 100 is about 20 yards when you factor in the turns. Given these differences, the long-course peak preparation cannot be as long as the short-course taper.

Apparent Effect of the Season's Training

If an athlete is swimming slowly as you near peak preparation, it may be necessary to taper the swimmer longer or more drastically. Swimmers will adapt to the stress placed on them in training to different degrees. Your evaluation of a swimmer's need for additional rest may be critical for success at the championship meet.

More Rest, Not More Work

When in doubt during peak preparation planning, a good general rule is to do less and not more. Coach Dean Hawkes, Kelly

Walsh High School in Casper, Wyoming, commented to me on winning their school's first boys' state championship in 37 years that he rested his sprinters the most ever to achieve that championship. I have known coaches that increased bed rest as well as decreasing swimming intensity and distance for one or two weeks to bring their athletes back to championship form.

One of my Olympic swimmers rested for one week after a rather slow relay swim at the start of the Olympic Games swim events. For one week, she did drill swimming only, low yardage, and a few 10-meter speed bursts, plus extra bed rest. At the end of the week, she won a gold medal and set a new world record in the 100-meter backstroke.

This was necessary on a large number of occasions during my coaching career, and it was always successful. More work never produced the desired results when the swimmer wasn't producing successful times during peak preparation or in competition.

Swimmer's Age

Always taper older swimmers longer than younger ones. Mature men and women need a longer taper than high school swimmers, and high school swimmers can taper longer than younger swimmers.

Younger age-group swimmers don't respond in the same manner as older swimmers to the normal taper process. Leading up to the competition, these young athletes should swim fast in practice and have short peak preparation periods. Young age-group swimmers may respond psychologically in a peak preparation period, but don't expect a major physiological adjustment to their taper; for one thing, they have less muscle mass, and for another, they don't get as tired as mature swimmers during training.

When in doubt during peak preparation planning, a good general rule is to do less and not more.

Intensity of Training in Peak Preparation

Control the intensity according to those same factors that you considered to determine the length of the peak preparation. You must individualize your training schedule to a high degree at this stage of the season. I have had as many as eight different workout groups preparing for a state high school championship. In my final preparation, the fewest number of groups has been three. Every swimmer must believe that the taper is designed specifically for him or her.

It can't become a question of coach convenience; the best swimmer preparation must be the controlling factor. Conducting several taper groups requires more time and planning from the coach. When I had many taper groups, I needed an additional hour of planning time each day. I also needed more time to communicate to my assistant coach and to my student managers the details of the plan and how they fit into it.

Organization was the key. Every assistant and swimmer knew what had to be timed and when it would happen. I always staggered the timed swims so that every athlete received individual coaching attention at some point in the session.

The successful results of this special attention to my swimmers' specific preparation made any required extra coaching time more than worth the effort.

There must be some intensity training throughout peak preparation. Athletes must continue to know the feeling that comes from swimming fast. They just don't do as much of it, and what amount they do is highly specific to their events. Swimmers need to swim fast when called to do so and should lighten up appropriately as directed. You should reduce the swimmers' total yardage but have them maintain enough aerobic endurance on enough swims to hold their aerobic capacity through this period, and this will vary according to their specific events.

THE THREE RS

Coach Dave Haller, former Olympic coach of Great Britain and Hong Kong, spoke to my team just before our summer regional championship one season. He stated that peak performance should be expected if the work has been done during the season's training. Keep it simple. Peak performance is made up of the three Rs: rest, relax, and rehearse.

Rest is a patterned behavior, built on regular habits. If the swimmer is exceptionally tired, then more bed rest is essential. The swimmer must take care at the competition to maintain regular habits. It would be foolish for any swimmer to throw away months of intense training by losing focus close to the competition. This is no time for late nights or any other nonproductive behaviors.

Relaxation is essential for peak preparation. Swimmers should rest in a relaxed manner. They should put their minds at ease and not think of the competition. Stretching and loosening exercises help swimmers relax, as does playing games to get their minds free and easy.

Rehearsing is the third R. Swimmers should mentally rehearse the start and the entire swim, visualizing swimming fast yet easy. They should see themselves building their race, focusing on good turns, and having a strong finish. They should think about the crowd conditions and whatever else may be a factor in the competition. All of this is done in a relaxed manner.

A Thousand Times in Your Mind

One of our outstanding young men won the state championship in the 200 and 500 freestyle events in his senior year of high school. Each of his swims was a new national high school record. He defeated a rival who held the state records for these events and had been the previous state champion for several years. After the meet, a reporter asked him if he was surprised by his wins and record times. He answered, "I wasn't surprised because I had swum those races a thousand times in my mind." This is the result of relaxed rehearsal. The subconscious mind has already programmed the race.

PLANNING PEAK PERFORMANCE

I gave the following instructions designated throughout this section in a handout to the Tacoma Swim Club going into the peak preparation period prior to the region championship.

"The championship meet has been the driving force of our training efforts throughout this winter season. Each of our goals would ideally be attained in our championship meet swims. Championship meet time is fast approaching. What can we now do to enable each of us to swim at our best?

"Our training for the most part is over. Our endurance training will be maintenance work only from now on. Specific race pace swims to get sustained speed for our events will be the focus in our training."

Trip Preparation

Most of our championship meets involved a trip away from home. A swim meet away from home can be more tiring, because the swimmers will be sleeping in a different bed, making food choices from a restaurant menu, and having other distractions. "Focus through the complete championship. Many of us will have our best events on the last day. Get your needed rest and plan to have a curfew each evening. Get to bed each night as soon as possible after the competition. Plan a nap every day by getting back to your motel right after the preliminaries. Avoid getting trapped into a TV program that is beyond your rest time, and avoid any party atmosphere that depletes you before the competition is over."

Nutrition

"A lot of your eating will be snacking at the meet and in the motel, but you will also be making food selections from a menu. Plan ahead and, ideally, you shouldn't change your eating habits drastically. All through the season, I have encouraged you to eat nutritionally. If you plan ahead, you can maintain this through the meet. When you are doing less training, some of you will have to take smaller servings. Plan to bring healthy snacks only. Keep hydrated, and bring your water bottles to the meet. Keep them full and drink water or a diluted sports drink frequently."

Mental Rehearsal

"The mental part of competing is most important. Focus on what you plan to do. If you are mentally tough all the way through each event, you will achieve good results. Every race-pace swim in training and at the meet must be visualized as part of your swim. Count strokes for stroke efficiency, both in training and in the warm-up at the meet. See yourself swimming the event. Visualize a perfect start, a super breakout stroke to capture the momen-

tum of the dive, and an easy but fast swim with your planned breathing pattern. Focus on the wall and the turn as you approach each wall. Build your speed into each wall, swimming strongly to it, and see yourself turning fast. Kick and break off the wall, again capturing the speed from the momentum of the push-off. See yourself getting stronger and building your speed in the second half of the race. Visualize yourself at your fastest and strongest on the final portion of the race. See yourself concentrating on the final wall and the finish.

"Stay positive and tough. Cheering for your teammates is very important. When we cheer together and recognize the great performances, we give ourselves the best chance to be successful. MENTAL GIANTS or mental midgets? The choice is with each of us. Let's go for it!

"We are going into something special in peak preparation. Peak preparation requires some intense and focused swimming. We need some of the most race-specific swims of the

season at this time, and they don't always come easily. You won't be great every day during this period of time. Your body will be adapting, so just be sure that your mind is adapting too by being positive. The objective is to be great on race day.

"The extra rest that you may be able to get in these final weeks will benefit you, so you must plan on nap time on weekends and avoid late nights from now on, including weekends. Talk to the coach if you have any questions or concerns."

PREPARING THE RELAY TEAMS

Relays make swimming more of a team sport. Some athletes surpass their best times only when swimming relays, and some swimmers will always produce relay times that are at least as good as their individual race times. Some swimmers will produce personal best swims only in individual events. Because of these many possibilities, you need to know your swimmers and what to expect from them in relay swims.

Relays are exciting events, and it is not unusual to have the lead change several times during the race. High school swim meets begin and end with relays. They start with a 200-yard medley relay and end with a 400-yard free relay. Within the meet, there is also a 200-yard free relay. The USA Swimming National Championship meets have three relay events, the 400 and 800 freestyle relays and the 400 medley relay. These relays will be measured in meters in the long-course championship and in yards in the short course.

Instructions to the Relay

I love coaching relays, because they bring a team together and draw a lot of fan focus. I instruct my relay team members on the importance of the event. If it is the first event, I want them to think about getting our entire team hyped on their initial success.

I talk about team pride to our relay members. I tell them that it takes four swimmers to win a relay. I also tell them what I expect from them in order to win the relay event. Each must contribute his or her best in order for the final swimmer to be in a position to win.

I talk about our relay team tradition and about what a great relays we've had both at Wilson High School and on Tacoma Swim Club. Remind swimmers to talk to each other on the blocks. The last swimmer must encourage the other three, while the first must inspire the others by his or her swim and by verbally encouraging the other relay members.

Position on the Relays

Position your relay members according to the strengths of the swimmers and the distance of the relay event. The medley relay consists of four athletes who each swim a different stroke in the following order: backstroke, breaststroke, butterfly, and freestyle. The freestyle relay consists of four athletes who each swim crawl.

Medley Relays

You will usually go with your best swimmer in each of the four different strokes if they are available. Sometimes it is necessary to hold one or more of your best stroke swimmers out of the medley relay in order to have them available for a freestyle relay later in the meet. In high school and college swimming, the medley relay is usually the first event. In the short 200 medley relay, each swimmer swims a 50 segment. In very short relays, I believe in getting out in front, because it takes a very strong swimmer to come from behind in a short relay.

Go for very fast backstroke and breaststroke legs on a 200 medley relay. When the relay is out front and has some open water, the butterfly and/or the freestyle legs can be slightly weaker. When the team is out front, the final legs will have smoother and faster water to swim in. This is a good position, psychologically, for your weaker swimmers to perform at their very best.

An Important Event

My Wilson High School teams always tried to win the 200-yard medley relay in the state championship meet, because it was the first event and provided a big mental boost to start the meet if they won.

I would always place strong backstroke and breaststroke swimmers in the front two positions. I often held my best flyer and/or my best freestyle swimmer for the free relay. Year after year, our number two flyer or an even weaker freestyle swimmer would turn in a super swim to win the 200 medley relay.

Because it is longer, the 400 medley relay provides time for a good inside swimmer to bring this event from behind. I do not always emphasize getting out front with the first swimmers in this event, but I prefer using at least my best swimmers in the backstroke, breaststroke, and butterfly legs. You can get by with a weaker freestyle leg when you are strong in the first three.

Freestyle Relays

You have more options for the relay order in freestyle relays, because each swimmer normally swims the crawl stroke. You must decide which order is best for different situations. Your options would include swimming 1, 2, 3, 4, which would be the fastest swimmer to the slowest. The more traditional order of relay swimmers is either 1 or 2 in the first position, 4 in the second, 3 in the third, and 1 or 2 in the anchor leg. You might use several other options depending on a number of other considerations. For example, if one swimmer came off of a preceding event, you might place her or him in a different relay position than you would have otherwise.

In the 200 free relay, which is short, I like my swimmers to get out front, if possible, for the fastest and smoothest water. Also, other teams must swim in your wake. I like a 1, 2, 3, 4 order in this relay.

In the 400 freestyle relay, I like to use a little more variety in the order. I use a 1, 4, 3, 2 or a 2, 4, 3, 1 most frequently. I will also use a 1, 2, 3, 4 order in this relay for some of the same reasons that I would in the 200 freestyle relay.

When we have a less than average chance to win a 400 relay, I like a 1, 2, 3, 4 order that attempts to break the other relay teams' will to win. If you get out front by as big a margin as possible, it makes it look extremely difficult to catch up. You can also pump up your anchor swimmer to make the swim of his or her life in this situation.

The 800 freestyle relay is another story, because it is long enough for each swimmer to come from behind during each 200 leg. Consequently, I may use any relay order to best fit the situation.

I prefer an experienced and very strong anchor swimmer in the 800. An experienced fourth athlete will swim the full 200 strong and in control, which is very important when the swimmer dives in behind another relay. He or she must "reel in" the swimmer in front and not overswim the first part of the 200 trying to overtake the leading swimmer too quickly. Also, when the anchor swimmer is ahead and must hold off a very fast swimmer from the team behind, he or she must not overswim the first part of the relay but save enough to finish strongly.

SUMMARY

Preparing for meets requires planning, and it is not the same procedure for every meet. The following points need to be considered:

1. Your major preparation should be for your championship meet.
2. All meets must contribute to preparation for the championship.
3. There are several types of in-season meets, and some may be more important than others.

4. The length of your peak preparation or taper will depend on a number of factors:

   • Males should taper longer than females.

   • Sprinters should taper longer than distance swimmers.

   • Heavily muscled swimmers should taper longer than slight or average swimmers.

   • Swimmers should taper longer for a short championship meet than for a long championship meet.

   • Swimmers should taper longer for a short-course meet than a long-course meet.

   • Highly trained and stressed swimmers should taper longer.

   • Older swimmers should taper longer than younger swimmers.

   • The taper should also depend on the swimmer's individual history.

5. Individualize your workouts in the taper.

6. Remember the three Rs: rest, relax, and rehearse.

7. Relays are a special focus in any meet.

8. Consider several factors when determining the order of your relay swimmers.

Chapter 14

HANDLING MEETS

Coach but don't overcoach. In other words, avoid overcoaching at the competition, because too many instructions will overload and confuse your swimmers. Let them go out and compete, and then you can do the necessary coaching in your next practice sessions.

I keep my instructions at the competition short and to the point, because swimmers can only focus on a few items when competing. I believe that a brief reminder regarding race control and sustained speed is a lot of coaching before an event.

BE A COACH, NOT A CRITIC

As a coach, be positive and try to avoid telling swimmers what they are doing wrong. You want to create a correct picture in their minds, so avoid negative images. Make your postevent evaluation brief and try to create a positive mental picture for the swimmer whenever possible. Say things like "Great race! I loved your finish!" or "Your stroke tempo was right on!" Any one of these may be enough coaching after an event in competition.

Avoid telling a swimmer that he or she destroyed the third turn or crashed on the back half of the race, because these are negative statements that create the wrong pictures in a swimmer's mind. They already know what they did wrong. Your job is to erase these pictures, not to perpetuate them. For instance, tell your swimmers to focus more on their buildup into the walls, and they will have stronger turns; tell them to be fast and easy with regular breathing cycles early in their race, and they will have a much stronger back half in their next swim. Brief and concise statements that are familiar work best. Tell swimmers what they have already heard from you during practice, because it will be comfortable to them and they can more easily process it. In short, be a coach and not a critic.

A Prelim to Final Adjustment

Many times a simple adjustment from a prelim swim to finals is appropriate. I've watched my swimmers go out on the first 100 of a 200 out of control and too fast and then drop an anchor during the second 100. The opposite happens as well: a too slow first 100 and then too little too late for the finish. A brief analysis after the prelim swim will often put your swimmer on the right track for a much better swim in the finals. I have experienced three- to four-second improvements in final swims when the swimmer makes a positive adjustment.

REGULAR SEASON MEETS AND MAJOR MEETS

Dual and regular season meets prepare the team for the championship meets and are the purest form of training. During a practice session, it is impossible to completely duplicate the race-pace speed and competitive circumstances that exist in actual competition.

Correct your swimmers' racing mistakes during the dual meets and other regular season meets, because this is the time to learn how the swimmers race best. The dual meet season is your testing and learning period prior to the championship.

The Warm-Up

Teach the value of a good warm-up during the regular competitive season. Swimmers must know their best warm-up before the champi-onship meet, so they will have more confidence when going into their most important meet of the season.

The warm-up has two phases. In the first, the primary concern is to loosen up and to feel comfortable in the water. The second is designed to prepare the swimmer's muscles, circulatory system, and nervous system for the major physical effort necessary in the event.

During the first part of the warm-up, athletes should swim a moderate, easy crawl. Emphasize a long streamlined glide off each wall. Swimmers must listen to their bodies and get a feel for the water, and they should avoid racing during this phase of warm-up.

Next, swimmers need to begin to include the best in basic technique. Include stroke drills and count the number of strokes per length in this phase. Gradually increase the swimmers' intensity and heart rate by doing some race-pace 50s or 100s. Having swimmers dive 25, or 12-1/2, may also be necessary for the sprint events. Finally, a brief cool-down should have the swimmer ready for competition.

The warm-up for competition is highly individualized. Swimmers must learn to understand their own bodies to maximize the chances for success from a good warm-up. The purpose of a warm-up is preparing to swim fast, and the quality of a warm-up can make or break a good performance. Warm-ups are not the time to socialize and to cut corners, so swimmers must use them wisely.

After the warm-up, I advise my swimmers to dry off and to stay warm by wearing dry socks, shoes, and sweat suits. In some outside conditions, parkas and gloves may be necessary.

If the main warm-up was concluded a long time before the swim, it may be necessary to loosen up again briefly prior to the competition. Swimmers should evaluate whether they need to return to a water warm-up prior to the swim. If the time period is less than 45 minutes or so, swimmers can decide if moving and stretching will be enough preparation or if they need to return briefly to the water. When the waiting time is over one hour, I usually advise a brief return to the water to loosen up.

The Cool-Down

Have your swimmers take the time to cool-down sufficiently after their events. Just after their event, they should do some easy swimming in the main pool or a warm-up pool.

Swimming down in this manner will disperse the lactic acid that has accumulated in the muscles after racing. Swimmers who cool down will have a much better chance to be successful in the meet's next race.

HOME VERSUS AWAY

Training is usually reduced on the day you travel to a meet, because of the added time needed to travel. If the meet is during the regular season, then you should attempt to schedule enough pool time to keep your swimmers aerobically fit.

Swimmers traveling by van or automobile will need to stretch out and walk around during stops. For longer trips, I recommend a stop every hour.

Riding in a van or automobile provides swimmers with additional rest. Sitting may be uncomfortable, but it does conserve energy, which is an important factor in each swimmer's favor at the competition.

An Early Coaching Experience

One year we traveled by automobiles for two and a half days on a trip to California. Over that time we drove about 20 hours, and we slept out on the ground each night. The only swim we took on the trip was a recreational one in a freshwater lake. Basically, the swimmers were locked up in a car for more than 2 days, resulting in a "forced rest." We had one night's rest in a motel before starting a major three-day meet.

The results were excellent; most everyone swam personal best times in their events. The forced rest seemed to be the best explanation for our success.

A Time Zone Change

Air travel often requires a change in time zones, so ask swimmers to begin adapting to the time zone change prior to departure. Within the continental United States, your time zone change may be one, two, or three hours.

If it is a one-hour time change, swimmers should go to bed and arise one hour earlier or later depending on the direction traveled. If it is a two- or three-hour change, gradually alter the bedtime hours over the course of a week. I also adjust our practice schedule so that it is as close as possible to the same time schedule of the competition in the different time zone.

When competing in the same time zone, I am comfortable traveling up to the day before the meet, but when a change of zone is required, I prefer traveling a minimum of one day earlier than the day before for each hour of time zone change.

If we could not afford to travel several days early, then I would convince my swimmers to adjust to the new time zone prior to departure for the best results. Nine times out of ten, believing makes the adjustment work.

The Away Environment

Dual meet competition at a traditional rival's pool requires some special coaching. Visualizing the environment, including the spectator involvement, can help prepare the team.

Before we depart for a meet, I want my swimmers prepared for the home team's band, their cheerleaders, and their crowd's enthusiasm. Stories of past swim meets can do much to have your team ready for the unexpected.

Expect the Unexpected

In my first year at Wilson High School, we swam an away meet at a 20-yard pool. It was the first dual meet of the season that Wilson had lost, and we only lost two dual meets in 25 years. I considered it a disaster because I had not prepared our team for a tough meet in a hostile environment and in a shorter pool. I learned from this experience.

Some meets are in communities that have a strong spectator backing. The ability of the swimmers to keep their heads and to maintain focus will make the difference between winning and losing. Nothing quiets hostile fans quicker than swimming fast and competing tough.

You should always expect the unexpected. You are going to lose team points on a disqualification occasionally. If automatic timing isn't available, you may lose some close races. However, if you keep the team focused, you can weather adversity.

We rehearse as many of the meet conditions as possible before we travel to an away meet. Pictures of the pool or previous videotapes of meets in the pool will help to prepare swimmers.

State Meets in the University of Washington Pool

When I coached Wilson High School, the state meets used to be held in the University of Washington pool. The pool was built in the 1930s and had tile turning lines that were extremely narrow, half the width of today's standard lines. It wasn't a turning T but rather just a line on the bottom and end walls.

I had our shop teacher make a sheet metal copy of the university's turning line. He painted it white with a black line the same size as that at the university. It hung from our pool gutter and covered our own turning T completely.

We practiced on those improvised turning lines for the final few weeks of our season. Consequently, we were always ready for the turning walls at the University of Washington.

Individual Readiness

I have stated frequently in this book that our team's physical readiness depended on the stage of the season. If you stick to your season plan, you will be physically prepared at the championship meet, with the possible exception of illness and injury.

Swimming is a technique-driven sport, and as a result, some swimmers may need to refocus on technique. An individual swimmer may need some stroke adjusting at a particular time to compete successfully, so be prepared to coach technique when necessary to help a swimmer improve. Refocusing on technique can help the swimmer maintain self-confidence. I believe that you must tell swimmers what you expect from them in competition, because it provides them with direction and realistic expectations.

Personal Conduct

Swimmers must learn to be proud of their good efforts in competition as well as in practice. Whether they win or lose, swimmers should act with class. Congratulating opponents after a race should be a habit.

We played some very important and fun games at Wilson High School that effectively taught us better habits both in practice and competition.

Turkey Talk

Every Thanksgiving season, I would introduce our Wilson High School team to "turkey talk." We used a number of descriptive terms to establish the basic premise that turkeys were dumb birds. Swimmers would lose points on their season chart for any "turkey" acts during the season.

One or more of the following would qualify a swimmer for the rank of turkey: a swimmer who neither warms up nor cools down; a swimmer who loses count of the number of lengths completed in a race; a swimmer who practices slow turns; a swimmer who false starts out of an event; a swimmer who coughs, cries, moans, or grimaces at the end of a race or sprints the last 15 yards of a longer race after taking a bath through the preceding sections; anyone who talks a lot and walks a lot in practice or in premeet warm-up; and, finally, anyone who stops a lot, especially in midpool. I told my swimmers that turkeys gather in flocks and that if one turkey stops, all the others will stop to find out why the first turkey stopped.

Punker Chatter

The second name game we played applied more closely to competitive situations than the turkey game. I tried to encourage individual responsibility through the punker game by subtracting points on our master motivational chart from anyone who earned punker status.

One of our posters read, "A punker always has a good excuse." I would list the number of good excuses that I had heard in my coaching career. It would usually total two, one I heard maybe 20 years earlier and another only 5 years ago. The idea of the game was to give swimmers little opportunity to make excuses for a poor effort or performance. I wanted them to make their own choices and to take responsibility for the consequences of their actions and eliminate excuses.

Our name games taught swimmers some good competitive habits and how to handle adversities like defeat or a poor swim. These were used only with our high school boys' teams, and they had fun with the games and learned from them. I didn't use this name game with age-group swimmers or our senior female swimmers. I questioned the perceived negativity that may have resulted within these groups.

Strategic Decisions

You will make most of your decisions on who will swim each event before the meet. Yet, there are always some swimmers who are probable in a particular event. In dual meets, this flexibility is possible, but in championship meets, you can't usually make changes. An upset in one event and a score differential may necessitate a lineup change in midmeet in a dual meet.

Before the meet, prepare your team for the possibility of lineup changes. For example, you might say that Jim will swim the 200 freestyle and the 100 butterfly, unless the score indicates otherwise after the first relay. Jim may swim the 200 individual medley or the 100 freestyle if necessary. Such foresight on the coach's part will prepare Jim and his teammates for this possibility.

Explain the reasons for your lineup choices when you announce them to your team, because they need to understand them in order to feel a part of the decision. Sometimes they need to have direct input into their event selection, particularly for the championship meet.

More Than One Winner

I always held a meeting with each swimmer to pick the events that she or he would swim at the championship meet. I always sought to balance team need with individual choice.

In one state high school championship, I had my four best freestyle swimmers select the 200 free as one of their best events. I then pointed out to each of them that we now had our four best swimmers in the same event. They all looked me in the eye and said, "I can win, coach." Because the outcome of the meet was not in doubt, I said to each of them, "Go for it."

The event was loaded with the best talent in the state. Our four boys went a very close 1, 2, 3, and 4 in the event, all at personal best times. They were all winners on that day and I have always respected them for the courage of their convictions.

Premeet Talks

In a regular season meet, I talk to my swimmers about team and individual pride. I tell them that they can always race tough, even if they can't race fast. I let them know that I

expect an honest effort in each of their races, without any special rest or taper. Usually, you do not need to do more than this.

For the regular season meet exception, I talk in much the same way, but I tell them I expect them to reach a little deeper for this special occasion. If we have a morning or two off from training, I will remind them of it and will suggest that they should be better than usual.

I also ask them to focus on sustained speed. All meets are a dress rehearsal for the championship, and we will be our best when we can hold our speed through the middle and the finish of our races. I may ask them to predict their race times and split times, because this helps maintain focus.

I discussed the championship meet talk already in chapter 13, under peak preparation. Personal pride, team pride, and sustained speed continue to be points of emphasis throughout the championship meet.

Running Score

Have one of your managers keep a running score throughout the meet to ensure that no clerical error occurs. Any discrepancy must be reported to the coach immediately.

Split Times

After every event, you must record your swimmers' split times. Stroke counts and stroke rates are also valuable information for each event, and we record this whenever possible. Each swimmer should go over the split times to better prepare for the next race.

Postmeet Team Meeting

When you win, the postmeet team meeting should be held the next day, because it will likely be more effective after the natural high of winning abates. On the other hand, when you lose, you should have your team meeting right after competing. Don't let the team dwell on a loss; they need their coach at this time to focus on the bright spots and on the future.

The Second Dual Meet Loss

Wilson High School lost its second dual meet in my last year of coaching, 24 years after the first loss. I talked to the team immediately after the meet and told them that I was proud of them and nothing had changed. I let them know that we were on schedule and headed for a great state championship. It was the right timing given the situation.

SUMMARY

When coaching meets, you must adhere to some basic principles, such as the following:

1. Avoid overcoaching.
2. Focus on a few specific points.
3. Coach in a positive way.
4. Use brief and concise statements because they work best.
5. Correct mistakes during the regular or dual meet season.
6. Teach an effective warm-up to your swimmers.
7. Make sure warm-ups are individualized.
8. Have swimmers cool down sufficiently after racing.
9. Adjust for time zone changes prior to departure.
10. Prepare for the away meet environment.
11. Tell your swimmers what you expect from them.
12. Teach proper personal conduct.
13. Give your swimmers some say in their event selection.
14. Be there for your team when they lose.

Part V

COACHING EVALUATION

Chapter 15

EVALUATING SWIMMERS' PERFORMANCE

You should constantly evaluate your swimmers and your own coaching. I want to know how my swimmers are adapting to my training program. I may evaluate the results of our endurance training weekly or over a period of several weeks. However, I evaluate each swimmer's progress in stroke technique daily.

Always base your evaluations on the swimmers' individual abilities and starting point. Don't judge the average swimmer based on the performance of the best swimmer.

The Last Can Be First

In practice, my most glowing evaluation will often go to my slowest swimmer. When one of our lowest level swimmers does his or her best set of repeat swims in practice, I focus the spotlight on that person, because such recognition for practice effort always inspires our entire team, especially when it comes to one of the lower level swimmers.

I base my preseason evaluation on, first, the swimmer's attendance, and second, his or her work habits, both of which are necessary early steps for helping the swimmer adapt both physically and mentally to the training.

PRACTICES

It is the will to prepare to win that counts. Through success in practice, swimmers attain mental toughness and confidence. I think of each practice session as an opportunity for swimmers to invest in their own success; they will get out of their competitions only what they put in during the practices. Practices offer the coach the opportunity to establish baseline performance levels for swimmers and then evaluate their progress.

Observations

Observe your swimmers in practice and require good technique from them even when they are tired from training. Continue to teach basic skills in all practice sessions, watching for fast turns, streamlined push-offs, and distance per stroke. Swimmers doing great things and doing them right in practice will be dynamite in competition.

I watch my swimmers from as many angles as possible during practice—from the side of the pool, at the end of the lane (the swimmer both coming and going), overhead, and underwater. Find a high overhead view for an excellent position to evaluate technique.

Whenever possible, you should also observe your swimmers underwater. Take advantage of underwater observation windows when they are available, or go into the water with a face mask, if that is the only thing available. I used a face mask one workout per week in most of my high school coaching. Underwater taping is very valuable and should be used when the opportunity is available.

Look at your swimmers from an upside down viewpoint by lowering your head and looking under your armpit. If you lean over slightly with your back to the pool, you will see more and enhance your understanding of how the water flows off the swimmer's arms and around the body. Strange as this might sound, I guarantee that it works.

Recognize when your swimmers are "stale" from training by observing their performance levels. When practice has deteriorated to the point that most team members have lost their enthusiasm, it is time to make a change in your coaching approach. One thing to do is introduce some fun into the training by lightening up your approach and creating some excitement through change. Take a day off from training if necessary. Training results will soon improve again when you do this.

Record Keeping

Keep a record of daily attendance, because success in competition usually correlates with good attendance. Often, attendance records can help explain the success or failure of any particular swimmer. Individual conferences with a swimmer will benefit from a record of that swimmer's attendance. A written attendance record can jolt a swimmer into reality because swimmers often don't realize that a lack of attendance can be at the root of a performance problem.

I make a written log of all my training sessions, and these are based on my season plan, as I outlined it in chapter 11. This log gives me an accurate record of exactly what each swimmer did in training day by day.

Record your swimmers' practice times every day whenever appropriate. For each main set, swimmers report their times from the pace clocks at the ends or sides of the pool. Swimmers must learn how to do this accurately. Occasionally, every swim is hand-timed. Recording the practice times motivates swimmers, and you will have a written record to refer to when necessary. You can measure in your written log both the intensity of the training and the swimmer's success in training.

I also record the swimmer's heart rate on some of the training sets. The swimmers usually count their own heart rate, but I have also used a heart rate monitor for more accuracy. By monitoring heart rate, you can also tell when a swimmer is failing to adapt to particular training sets.

Both practice times and heart rates can indicate the degree of the swimmer's adaptation to training. If a swimmer is failing to adapt, you can take steps quickly to correct it.

Whenever possible, I like to record the stroke count per 50 in race-pace sets. I also record stroke rate in race-pace sets to indicate the proper stroke tempo for each swimmer. I use a special stroke rate watch that gives me the number of strokes per minute.

Both practice times and heart rates can indicate the degree of the swimmer's adaptation to training.

MEETS

As I stated previously, I consider meets the purest form of training. Competition results should not be measured in individual wins or losses. Meets are a learning experience, and it is up to you as the coach to ensure that they are positive.

Observations

Observe your swimmers to determine the weaknesses to improve and the strengths to praise. Record segments of the race that will enable the swimmer to train and race better in the future.

Watch each of your swimmers during the competition. I look for aggressiveness, stroke count, stroke rate, race pace, race tactics, breathing patterns, stroke technique, sustained speed, and the start, turn, and finish skills.

Aggressiveness, race tactics, breathing patterns, stroke technique, and start, turn, and finish skills are somewhat subjective to measure and require more coaching art, because you have to determine what and how much to throw at your swimmers.

Stroke count, stroke rate, split times, and sustained speed can be measured objectively for each swim. You can train managers and assistant coaches to do this job.

I can see more and better when I only observe the race, so I let my manager or assistant coach take split times. When I take split times, I miss too many technical aspects of the race. My attention needs to be focused only on the swim itself. I also like to use my swimmers who are not competing in that event to take turns taking the splits, because it gives them some ownership in the process and makes them more aware of the value of such records.

When free from recording and writing, I can talk to swimmers about the technical aspects of their races throughout the competition. I can go over split times and help each swimmer evaluate the race, and I can encourage and attempt to motivate swimmers when necessary.

Observing From Afar

Occasionally, I remove myself from the pool deck in a training type of swim meet. If I can sit in an elevated bleacher section, I can observe the swims much more accurately. I'm able to observe my swimmers and all of their racing weaknesses more clearly than at deck level. You should only take this approach in specific situations, and your team members need to know why you are doing it.

Record Times

Record split times for every event. When possible, record the stroke rate and the stroke count for each segment of the event. These records will be invaluable for your swimmers and yourself in planning for future improvement.

Examples of record forms for specific distances appear in figures 15.1 and 15.2. Make

copies of these records and give them to each swimmer, because they provide critical information for you and the swimmer. Split times that include the running time, the segment times, and the drop-off for the event are a minimum requirement. I recommend recording stroke rate and stroke count whenever possible.

SUMMARY

Evaluate your swimmers' performances both in practice and in competition. If you want change, then measure the results of both the practice sessions and the competition.

1. Coach with the belief that practices reflect the will of your team to prepare to win.
2. Observe your swimmers in practice from as many different angles as possible.
3. Require great technique in practice if you want it in competition.
4. Record daily attendance at your practice sessions.
5. Make a written log of each training session throughout the season.
6. Record the practice times and the heart rate for each swimmer in the main sets.
7. At the competition, delegate the taking and recording of split times and other information to others; this will permit you to focus on all aspects of each race.
8. Make a written record of split times and other information to discuss with each swimmer.
9. Give copies of the meet records to each swimmer.

Sample Record Form for Events Over Distances of 100 to 400 Yards or Meters

Event: _200 yard freestyle_____   Swimmer: _John Smith_____

Segments:	50	100	150	200	250	300	350	400
Split times:	_23.6_	_48.7_	_1:14.0_	_1:39.0_	___	___	___	___
Stroke rate:	_48_	_47_	_48_	_49_	___	___	___	___
Number of strokes:	_24_	_26_	_26_	_27_	___	___	___	___

Drop-off: 50 _____   50 _____ Total _____

100 _48.7_____   100 _50.3_____ Total _+1.6_____

200 _____   200 _____ Total _____

Figure 15.1 (a) Sample record form with data.

Event:_____   Swimmer: _____

Segments:	50	100	150	200	250	300	350	400
Split times:	___	___	___	___	___	___	___	___
Stroke rate:	___	___	___	___	___	___	___	___
Number of strokes:	___	___	___	___	___	___	___	___

Drop-off: 50 _____   50 _____ Total _____

100 _____   100 _____ Total _____

200 _____   200 _____ Total _____

Figure 15.1 (b) Blank record form.

Sample Record Form for Distances of 500 to 1650 Yards or 800 to 1500 Meters

	Running time	Segment 50s	Segment 100s	Segment 500/550s	Stroke rate	Stroke rate
50	_____	_____	_____	_____	_____	_____
100	_____	_____	_____	_____	_____	_____
150	_____	_____	_____	_____	_____	_____
200	_____	_____	_____	_____	_____	_____
250	_____	_____	_____	_____	_____	_____
300	_____	_____	_____	_____	_____	_____
350	_____	_____	_____	_____	_____	_____
400	_____	_____	_____	_____	_____	_____
450	_____	_____	_____	_____	_____	_____
500	_____	_____	_____	_____	_____	_____
550	_____	_____	_____	_____	_____	_____
600	_____	_____	_____	_____	_____	_____
650	_____	_____	_____	_____	_____	_____
700	_____	_____	_____	_____	_____	_____
750	_____	_____	_____	_____	_____	_____
800	_____	_____	_____	_____	_____	_____
850	_____	_____	_____	_____	_____	_____
900	_____	_____	_____	_____	_____	_____
950	_____	_____	_____	_____	_____	_____
1000	_____	_____	_____	_____	_____	_____
1050	_____	_____	_____	_____	_____	_____
1100	_____	_____	_____	_____	_____	_____
1150	_____	_____	_____	_____	_____	_____
1200	_____	_____	_____	_____	_____	_____
1250	_____	_____	_____	_____	_____	_____
1300	_____	_____	_____	_____	_____	_____
1350	_____	_____	_____	_____	_____	_____
1400	_____	_____	_____	_____	_____	_____
1450	_____	_____	_____	_____	_____	_____
1500	_____	_____	_____	_____	_____	_____
1550	_____	_____	_____	_____	_____	_____
1600	_____	_____	_____	_____	_____	_____
1650	_____	_____	_____	_____	_____	_____

Drop-off: (500) 250 _____   250 _____   Total _____
         (800) 400 _____   400 _____   Total _____

Segment split times: (1500/1650)
         500/550 _____   500/550 _____   500/550 _____

Figure 15.2 Sample record form.

Chapter
16

EVALUATING YOUR PROGRAM

Evaluate your program continuously, considering first whether you are still following your season plan. If you do this at least weekly throughout the season, you can determine if you need to make training adjustments in your season plan.

Of course, the major evaluation of your program must be made at the end of the season. Look at your program as soon as possible after the last championship meet, because that is the time when the results are most clear to you and your swimmers. Putting it aside until you are ready to deal with it may obscure some of the necessary details.

Make your evaluations as objectively as possible. You know when you have attained your goals and done the best that you were capable of.

Be honest in your self-evaluation. We have won at least one state championship meet where I knew that we had not done our best. The press and our boosters were most congratulatory over the fact that we had maintained our undefeated record and had won another consecutive championship meet.

However, I knew that we hadn't done our best, and my postmeet evaluation verified my feelings. We hadn't met the goals that we had set for ourselves. We had swum faster at the championship meet than our previous best, but not by much. From that evaluation, I made adjustments in planning for the next season, and it was a very successful one. We made major improvements again in our best times at the following state championship meet. A critical look at your own performance can keep you hungry and in high anticipation for the approaching new season.

As the saying goes, "If you are satisfied, you are finished." A kick in the pants delivered by yourself to yourself can keep you aimed in the right direction—up.

_____

A critical look at your own performance can keep you hungry and in high anticipation for the approaching season.

EVALUATING PERSONNEL

At the start of the season, swimmers listed their goals, and now, at the end, it is time to sit down with each swimmer and come to some conclusions. Did they reach their goals? Why did or didn't they reach them? This is a good time to help each swimmer learn how to set goals. In general, young inexperienced swimmers are more prone to set goals that are too difficult to reach in the short run. They are often in the "dream" phase of the goal-setting process.

Lost time from illnesses or injuries can be analyzed objectively at this time, as well as a review of the training that each swimmer accomplished. Write a statement for the swimmers based on your own evaluation first, and share with them any positive input.

Next, have your swimmers give their own personal views, so you can learn from them. Swimmers may have perceptions that are not valid, but if they believe them, you need to know. I like to have my swimmers complete a questionnaire prepared by me (see page 169). This is a good way to draw out information from the swimmers, especially the younger, inexperienced ones.

A copy of this questionnaire should be given back to each swimmer at the start of the next season when you are setting goals. The swimmers' self-evaluation will help them to better focus on the elements of success in their next season, and it will help you to remind them where they need to improve.

When you evaluate personnel, you aren't considering replacements unless you are able to recruit new swimmers (e.g., a college program might make a special effort to recruit a stroke swimmer). High school and club programs are usually limited to the swimmers available to them, and this limitation is generally based on geography.

Finally, you need to determine whether you have the swimmers in their best events both in the stroke and the distance. Make decisions that will place swimmers in their most effective events for the coming season.

EVALUATING STAFF

I was a head high school coach without an assistant for about 12 years. I was also without an assistant when I first started as a club coach. If you are the only staff member in your coaching situation, then you have to evaluate what you did best and assign student managers to do what work they can do. This will give you more time to do your coaching, as it did me.

I always evaluated my managers, and I liked to do it informally after practice. They would report the results of timed swims and other parts of the practice for which they were responsible, and then we would talk about what went well and what we needed to do better. I was never critical of these volunteer managers, and I always praised their contributions to the success of our team. My wife and I took them out to dinner on one special night every season.

If you have assistant coaches, you need to evaluate their performances to get the best from each of them. Evaluate your assistant coaches the same way that you do yourself. Delegate to them those duties that they do best and retain those that you do best. The bottom line is for you to have quality time to coach.

Make sure that your staff members understand their responsibilities and duties, and encourage assistants to develop a plan that will carry out their duties more effectively.

I prefer talking to my assistants in a postseason meeting that is social as well as businesslike. A dinner or lunch meeting at my expense is an ideal setting. In a relaxed and comfortable setting, we can review the effectiveness of our collective coaching.

Sample Questionnaire

"Build for the future by looking back"

Name: _____

1. Which goals did you achieve that you set for yourself this past long-course season?

2. Which goals did you not achieve that you set for yourself this past season?

3. Rate your effort in the following training areas this past season (score 0 to 10 with 10 as the highest possible score):

(a) _____ Stretching	(l) _____ Explosive speed sets	
(b) _____ Tubing	(m) _____ Race-pace sets	
(c) _____ Sled/bench	(n) _____ Anaerobic high quality sets	
(d) _____ Sit-ups/push-ups		
(e) _____ Attendance	(o) _____ Power rack sets	
(f) _____ Maintaining goal focus	(p) _____ Pulling sets	
(g) _____ Positive mental attitude	(q) _____ Sculling	
(h) _____ Regular season meet performance	(r) _____ Drills	
	(s) _____ Starts, turns, finishes	
(i) _____ Championship meet performance	(t) _____ Rest/sleep	
	(u) _____ Nutrition	
(j) _____ Endurance one (A.T.) sets	(v) _____ Kicking sets	
(k) _____ Aerobic endurance sets	(w) _____ Stroke count	

4. What did you do best, based on your scores and other areas that you feel are important?

5. What could you have done better, based on your scores and other areas that you feel are important?

6. Rate the following areas according to their importance for you to become the best that you can be in swimming (score 0 to 10 as before).

(a) _____ Mental approach to swimming	(f) _____ Hidden training (nutrition and rest)	
(b) _____ Goal setting	(g) _____ Handling adversity	
(c) _____ Following coach's training	(h) _____ Self-discipline	
(d) _____ Dry land training	(i) _____ Inner toughness	
(e) _____ Swimming training	(j) _____ Stroke technique	

Questions for discussion should include:

What responsibilities do you feel confident in performing?

What responsibilities do you feel the head coach must perform?

What were the strengths of our staff?

What were the weaknesses of our staff?

How was our communication? Did we always understand our daily, weekly, and season plans?

What suggestions would you make to make our coaching better?

These questions will provide a basis for positive input from your staff and will give you the opportunity to make suggestions to them. Take written notes of the meeting, and let your staff know that you value their input and that you intend to implement those suggestions that you mutually agree on.

Replace a staff member only when absolutely necessary. If your respective philosophies conflict, you might need to dismiss an assistant. Usually, however, I have to convince my low-paid assistant coaches to come back for another season, simply for the love of doing it.

EVALUATING EQUIPMENT

Evaluate the equipment that you are using at the end of each season. Are you using it most effectively? Do you need to make some changes in its use or perhaps in the equipment itself? Each year, there's new equipment on the market that you need to evaluate, because some of it may be a valuable addition to your program. I have added something new to our program every year. It keeps the program new and exciting for me and for the swimmers as well.

EVALUATING FACILITIES

Regardless of the number of facilities available to you, you must use what you have in the most effective manner. Never limit your ex-

pectations for swimming success on the available facilities. Swimmers who have set world records have had to do the bulk of their training in pools as short as 50 feet. What you do and how you do it is more important than where you do your training.

The ideal training facility would have space for dry land training, long-course and short-course training, and an area for very short pool training (35–50 feet). I have never had all of these available in any one facility. Most often, you will have to evaluate how you can better organize the use of your facility to get the most from it.

EVALUATING YOUR OWN PERFORMANCE

Judge your own performance as objectively as possible. Look at your season plan and evaluate it completely. (You should already have been making weekly evaluations throughout the season.) Now is the time to determine if your results at the championship meets indicate that it was the best plan.

You need to think about how the season plan could have been improved. I have never had a season where I wanted to do the very same thing again. Some adjustments always need to be made. Something can always be done better.

Evaluate the confidence of your swimmers in you. Do they trust your recommendations and your judgment? Are you secure in your decisions? Are you consistent in your discipline and in treatment of your swimmers? You are the rock on which your team is built. Were you that rock they needed at both the low and high points of the season?

Determine when and where you could have been better. Read and listen objectively to the evaluations of your swimmers and assistants. Act on their suggestions but avoid reacting. You have the opportunity to become a better coach by listening to your swimmers and assistants.

In addition to the questions already listed, consider scoring yourself on the following points when you evaluate yourself:

1. Your positive outlook
2. Your mental focus
3. Your communication with swimmers
4. Your communication with parents
5. Your use of your staff
6. Your consistency in teaching
7. Your ability to keep everything in perspective
8. Your ability to keep your program both challenging and fun

You can learn from your swimmers and your staff by asking them to evaluate you. You can learn a lot from their questionnaires at the season's end. You can even go beyond this and ask them to rate you in many of the same areas on the questionnaire. I have done this, and you can always learn from their input.

Deflating My Ego

I have received more than a few jolts in my self-perception as a coach from questionnaires that I have given to my swimmers. In my experience, most of the questionnaire feedback has been positive and has reinforced the direction and methods of my coaching. However, I have had responses from swimmers who thought that I didn't like them. Nothing could have been further from the truth, and we worked it out satisfactorily after talking.

As a result of these misunderstandings, I have become more sensitive to the feelings of the young athletes that I coach. I have learned to recognize more of the misconceptions of my athletes and to make the necessary corrections before major problems erupt.

Evaluating Your Own Goals

Determine where you did and didn't meet your own goals. Were they too high or too low? Were they specific enough? Whatever your answers to such questions, always strive to measure your goals accurately.

By using these evaluations, you can begin to set your goals for the next season.

Making Changes

After your evaluations, make decisions that will have a positive effect on your program in the coming season. Don't wait to make these decisions; tackle them immediately after the end of the season.

For example, after evaluating one of our team's long-course season results, we determined that much of our success was the result of adding speed work every day. It was the only major change that we had made during the season, and our results had improved dramatically. I added daily speed work over very short distances to all of our subsequent seasons with excellent results.

No evaluation process in itself can make changes. You have to be willing to follow the guidelines that result from the evaluation process in order to better your program. To grow as a coach, you must be somewhat flexible when it comes to improving the program. This seems to be a general trend among the better programs nationally and worldwide.

Correcting Problems

Sit down with your staff, the team, each swimmer individually, their parents, the administrators, and anyone else necessary to correct problems. Talk to them sometimes as a group and sometimes individually, one on one. Everyone wants to be and do better, and now is the time to agree on the best future plan of action.

The human side of any problem equation is the most challenging to correct. When everyone understands the situation clearly and works together to correct the problem, your next season has a much better chance for success.

Problems with equipment, facilities, and other items are easier to correct, because you can readily make decisions usually without treading on human emotions. However, it still may be best to discuss changes, so that every team member understands the reasons for them.

Building Stronger for the Future

Once you've evaluated all aspects of your program and made your decisions regarding changes, it is time to enthusiastically anticipate the next season. Swimmers will have received their own self-evaluations back from you at the start of the new season, and this should make them more aware of the ingredients for success.

Sell your new season's program through your enthusiasm. Let everyone know the part they played in planning for the new season through their season-end questionnaires.

Summary

1. Conduct your major program evaluation after the last championship meet.

2. Have your swimmers complete a prepared questionnaire at the end of the season.

3. Evaluate your assistant coaches' performance as well as your own.

4. Evaluate new equipment that may be needed, and determine the effectiveness of the old equipment.

5. Realize that your chances for success do not depend on the facility available to you.

6. Correct those problems that have been identified.

7. Determine changes for the next season from your evaluation process.

INDEX

Note: The italicized *f* and *t* following page numbers refer to figures and tables, respectively.

A

approaches for communication
    community support 17
    effective communication 9
    enthusiasm 9, 10
    honesty 13
    media attention 16-17
    motivation 9
    tips 13

B

backstroke
    arm stroke and coordination 80
    correct timing 75
    finishes 86
    optimizing distance per stroke 78
    positions 76-77
    relaxation and rotation 75, 76
    rhythm 75
    technique, summary of 82-83
    turns 86
backstroke, arm drills
    backstroke swims with plastic purse on forehead 81
    corkscrew drills 82
    double arm stroking 81
    double bent arm stroke finishes 80
    double bent arm stroke for back half 80
    fist drills 82
    one-arm swims with opposite arm carried above shoulder 81
    one-arm swims with opposite arm stationary at side 81
    persistence 82
    single bent arm finishes 81
    single bent arm strokes for back half 81
    spin-out drills 82
    swim the rope 82
    touch and go 81
    touchdown swims 81
backstroke, back starts
    categories of 83, 85
    positions 84-85

backstroke, optimizing distance per stroke
    backstroke flutter kick 78
    body position 78, 78*f*
    kicking 78
backstroke flutter kick drills
    arms overhead in torpedo kick on back 79
    cross-pool kicking underwater 79
    kicking with arms at side 79
    kicking with arms at side using trunk rotation 79
    kicking with arms folded behind head using trunk rotation 79
    kicking with arms overhead using trunk rotation 79
    one arm extended and one arm at side in trunk-rotated position 79
Barrowman, Mike 87
Benner, Jay 116, *xi*
Blanchard, Kenneth 22, 46
Block, George 53, 67, 95
Bottom, Mike 123
Bowman, Bob 54
breaststroke
    combination drills 95
    finishes 100
    starts 98
    summary of 95
    teaching, sequence of 91
    turns 98-100
    underwater pull-out drill 95, 96-97
breaststroke, kicking drills
    arms behind hips kicking 93
    arms extended streamlined kicking 92
    back breaststroke kick 92
    eggbeater kicking 92-93
    face down on pool deck 92
    kicking breaststroke with pull buoy 93
    launching drill 92
    sitting in gutter with legs in water 92
    slide/kick drill 93
    vertical kicking 92
    vertical kicking at wall 92

breaststroke, mechanics of
    streamlined position 88*f*
    wave style 87, 88
breaststroke, optimum distance per stroke
    feel of water 93
    sculling 93-94
breaststroke, stroke drills
    breaststroke with dolphin and breaststroke kick 94
    breaststroke with dolphin kick 94
    inner tube pulling 94
    one-arm swims 94
    pulling over lane line 94
    pulling with flutter kick 94
    pulling with head up 94
    shooters 95
    surf lane lines 94
    swim under rope 94
breaststroke, technical aspects of
    head and spine alignment 90*f*
    inward scull 88, 89-90
    outward scull 88, 89*f*
    points in teaching 90, 91
    reenter 89
breathing drills
    explained 66
    hand in pocket 67
    one-arm swims with nonstroking arm at side 66
    one-arm swims with one arm extended 66
    side glide delay 67
    stretch-up swims 66
    swim the rope 67
    thumb drag 67
butterfly
    basic arms 107
    distance and endurance considerations 106
    finishes 110
    Olympic Trials finalists 110
    sculling 45-46, 109
    special tips for teaching 106
    speed drill 109
    starts 110
    summary of butterfly 109-110
    teaching, sequence of 105-106
    transition drills 109
    turns 110
butterfly, drills
    extra kicks off walls 108
    jumping jack butterfly 108
    multiple kick butterfly 108
    one-arm swims with one arm at side 108
    one-arm swims with one arm extended 108
    vertical butterfly 109
butterfly, technique tips
    arm pull 104
    breathing 105
    entry 101, 104
    kicking 104-105
    positions 102-103
    recovery 104

butterfly, tips for teaching
    feel of water 106
    fins 106
    optimum distance per stroke 106
    paddle swims 106
butterfly kick
    body position 51-52
    the kick 53
    kicking drills 53-55
    leg position 53*f*
    streamlines, torpedo position 51, 52*f*

C
Cerutty, Percy 8
Churchill, Winston 13
club program. *See* program, club
coaching. *See* swimming coaches
communication
    community support 17
    effective communication 9
    enthusiasm 9, 10
    honesty 13
    media attention 16-17
    motivation 9
    tips 13
communication with others
    assistants 14
    media 16
    officials 13-14
    with other coaches 14
    with parents 14-15
    school faculty 15
    student body 16
communication with swimmers
    communication vs overreacting 12
    at competition 12-13
    early season communication 10
    effective communication 10
    needs, anticipating 10
    opportunities away from pool 12
    plateaus 10
    in pool 11, 12
    pool area team meetings 12
    setting schedule 10
    two-way communication 10-11
Counsilman, Doc 3-4, 12
crawl, drills for
    hand, wrist, elbow, emphasizing 64-65
    shark fin 66
    streamlined lateral kicking 65-66
    torpedo 65
crawl, sequence of teaching
    distance and endurance considerations 64
    explained 63
    fins 64
    special tips for crawl stroke 63-64
    waters awareness 64
crawl stroke
    breathing drills 66-67
    crawl stroke positions 62-63
    finishes 74

stroke mechanics 57
summary of 68
transition drills 67
turns 71-74
winning close races 74
crawl stroke, front starts
    crawl start, teaching tips for 71
    explained 68
    positions 69-70
    racing starts, improving 71
    starting signal, what to emphasize 68, 71
    swimmers' stance on blocks 68
    track start 71
crawl stroke, straight arm recovery for
    body position and streamlining 60
    crawl stroke positions 62-63
    the kick 61
    model for 60
    pressure points 60, 60*f*
    proper breathing 61, 63
    rotation and speed 60-61
crawl stroke, technical aspects
    arm stroke 58, 59, 59*f*
    body position 58
crawl stroke, turns
    drills to improve 71, 74
    positions 72-73
    steps in teaching 71

D
Daland, Peter 3
disciplinary action
    as learning experience 30
    responsibility 29
    standards vs rules 30
    suspensions 30
dolphin kick
    body position 51-52
    the kick 53
    kicking drills 53-55
    leg position 53*f*
    streamlined, torpedo position 51, 52*f*
Douglas, David 25
dry land training
    basic exercises 134-135
    medicine balls 134
    surgical tubing units 133-134
    swim benches or swim sleds 134

E
equipment. *See* training aids
Ervin, Anthony 123
evaluation of program
    after evaluations 172
    ego deflation 171
    end of season 167
    equipment 170
    facilities 170
    honesty 167
    personnel 168
    questionnaire, sample 171*f*

    season plan 167
    staff 168-170
    your own performance 170-171

F
fins, short 64, 82
Firby, Howard 4, 48, 60, 82, 104

G
goals, power of
    components of 24
    dreams into goals 26
    primary goal, focus on 25-26
    reasons leading to commitment 26
    setbacks and reaffirming goals 24
    setting swimmer goals 26
    visualizing gold 26-27
goals, results of. *See also* goal setting
    attaining and sustaining goals 28
    discipline 29
    leaders, building 28
    rewards 28
goal setting
    benefits of 27-28
    focus and setbacks 25
    principles of 25-26
    team goals 24-25
Goodel, Brian 26-27
Groovers and Grippers 64, 131

H
Hackett, Grant 58
Haines, George 3
Hall, Gary 123
Hall, Kaye 16, 27, 36-37, 47-48
Haller, Dave 115
hand paddles 82, 131
Han's Paddles 59, 63, 64, 131
Hawkes, Dean 144
high school program. *See* program, high school

K
Kenney, Skip 4
kickboard 55
kicking drills (dolphin or butterfly kick)
    back dolphin 54
    backstroke flag reach 55
    dolphin kick with arms at side 54
    front dolphin, hands back 55
    one-leg flutter kick to dolphin 54
    rockets 54
    teeter totter 53
    torpedo underwater kick 54
    vertical kicking 54

L
Leamy, Robin 58
Lincoln, Abraham 13
Lombardi, Vince 3, 28
Lorber, Robert 22, 46-47

M
Mauer, Lea 80
media
       acquiring cooperation of 16-17
       communicating with 16
meets, handling
       away environment 154
       cool-down 153
       dual and regular season meets 152
       early coaching experience 154
       expecting unexpected 154
       home vs away 153
       individual readiness 155
       keeping it simple 152
       positive postevent evaluations 151-152
       prelim to final adjustment 152
       state meets in Univ. of WA pool 154-155
       time zone changes 154
       warm-up 152-153
meets, personal conduct
       punker chatter 155-156
       turkey talk 155
meets, preparation for
       event, mental boost of winning 149
       freestyle relays 149
       peak performance 146
       peak preparation period 143-145
       programming the race 146
       relay teams 148-149
       team readiness 141-143
       three Rs 146
       trip preparation 146-148
meets, strategic decisions
       about 156
       all winners 156
       postmeet team meeting 157
       premeet talks 156
       running score 156
       second dual meet loss 157
       split times 156
Miller, Bob 4, 55
Morales, Pablo 110
motivational tools
       adversity and success 23-24
       books, tapes, and articles 23
       Fortune Cookie Corner 23
       inspiring experiences 24
       speakers 23
motivation for swimmers
       about 19, 20
       coach and swimmer motivation 20
       disciplinary action 29-30
       example from experience 27
       external influences 22-23
       goals, power of 24-27
       goals, results of 27-29
       monitoring process 27
       personal drive 21
       purpose, developing 20
       questionnaires 20-21
       sixth sense, developing 21
       sources of 21
       swimmers' development and success 22
       team aspect of swimming 19
       time standards 21-22

N
Nagy, Joseph 87
Nightingale, Earl 25-26

O
optimum distance per stroke drills
       minimum number drill 44
       race pace and stroke count 44-45
       speed and stroke length 45
       stroke rate 45
       stroking efficiency 44

P
performance, record keeping
       explained 162, 163
       meets 163
       observations 163-164
performance, (swimmers') evaluating
       observations 162
       observing from afar 164
       practices 162
       record keeping 162-164
       record times 164, 165*f,* 166*f*
       slowest swimmer, praising 161
philosophy, comfortable
       be yourself 5-6
       creating positive experiences 6
       eager to learn 6
       equal opportunity 6
philosophy, defining your
       change, adapting to 5
       key sources 4-5
       tenets for 5
philosophy, developing
       beliefs 3, 6
       believe and succeed 7
       learning opportunities 4
       origin of 4
       setting goals 7-8
       success, measuring 3
plan, developing
       ingredients of 114
       planning time period 113-114
plan, two-season yearly
       anaerobic and competition phase 117
       general endurance 116
       rest and peak preparation 117
       specific endurance 116-117
       supplemental considerations 117, 119
       training categories 117, 118*t*
       training sessions, sample 120-121
planning season, facilities
       additional needs 128
       changing pool structure 128
       medical precautions 128-129

nutritional guidelines 129
special interest display boards 128
water in pool and equipment 128
plans for training
aerobic training foundation 115-116
anaerobic/high school 121, 123
developing plan 113-114
general endurance/high school season 121
high school season calendar, example 122
master calendar 115
peak preparation/high school 123
planning yearly club training schedule 116
preparation, physical 123-124
qualifiers for national championship 115
specific endurance/high school season 121
specificity and individualization 123
15-week plan for typical high school season 124, 125*t*
winners and club swimmers 115
Potts, Debbie 78
practice, starting
getting too good 135
right on cards 135
special workouts 135-136
stacking kickboards 136
surf's up 136
three on two kickboards 136
tow your buddy 136
whirlpool 136
practices, preparation for
circle patterns 131, 131*f*
dry land training 133-135
facilities and pool setup 128-129
fun and effective practices 135
lanes, assigning 130-131
preliminary requirements 127-128
roster and events 129-130
special considerations 136-137
starting practice 135-136
training aids 131-133
training course 130
preparation, peak period
championship meet, length and type 144
doing less, not more 144-145
history of swimmer 144
length, deciding on 143
male or female 143
season's training, effect of 144
short or long course 144
sprint or distance swimmer 143-144
swimmer's age 145
swimmer's muscle mass 144
preparation, physical
about 123-124
strength 124
transition training 124
pressure points 79
program, club
club entry levels 34-35
fan support 36-37
financial support, gaining 35-36

recruiting swimmers 34
program, high school
faculty and administration support 33
fan support, establishing 36
financial support 33-34
recruiting swimmers 32
star attraction 36-37
team levels 32-33
program visibility, creating
cheering 38
pride in team, instilling 37-38
relays 39
steps for gaining 37
tradition 39
winning close races 38
Pursley, Dennis 115
Putting the One Minute Manager to Work (Blanchard, Lorber) 22, 46-47, 48

Q
Quick, Richard 4

R
Reese, Eddie 4
relay teams, preparing
instructions to relay 148
medley relays 148-149
position on relays 148
relays, about 148
Rogers, Will 16
roster and events
length of practice 129-130
setting up practice schedule 129

S
Schubert, Mark 4
sculling
benefits of 45
breaststroke position 46
extended sculling drill 94
hand paddles 45, 45*f*
other sculling positions 46
vertical inward sculling 93
Strangest Secret, The (Nightingale) 25-26
strokes, principles in teaching
drills 43
emphasizing teaching 46
fundamentals 43
increasing speed 44
learning by teaching 49
optimum distance per stroke drills 44-45
plateau, breaking out of 47, 48
resistance 44, 46
stroke coaching 48-49
stroke length, frequency and count 43
swimming speed 43
teaching, guidelines 46-47
Sweetenham, Bill 43, 44
Swim Coaching Bible, The (Bottom) 123
swimming coaches
opportunities of *xii*

resources *xi*
volunteer coaching *xi*
swimming program, building
about 31
club program 34-36
club swimming 31-32
high school program 32-34
other issues 36-37
program visibility, creating 37-39
trips 36

T
Tallman, John 4
team readiness
about 141-142
consistent training program 142
regular season meets, preparing for 142-143
training through meets 142
types of meets 142
Thornton, Nort 4, 44
Thorpe, Ian 58
Torres, Dana 123

training aids
goggles 132
hand paddles 131
kickboards 132
mirrors 132
miscellaneous aids 133
parachutes and buckets 133
power racks 133
pull buoys and inner tubes 132-133
rubber bands 132
swim fins 132
tethered swim belt and tubing 132
water bottles 132
transition drills
explained 67
optimum distance per stroke drills 44-45, 67
trip preparation
mental rehearsal 147-148
nutrition 146-147
Troy, Mike 12

W
Wood, Jim 24

ABOUT THE AUTHOR

Dick Hannula is one of the winningest high school and club coaches in the history of swimming, having racked up the longest high school undefeated streak on record, undefeated in 323 consecutive meets—including 24 consecutive Washington state high school boys' swimming championships. He is also one of the most respected coaches in swimming, having coached or consulted with teams from high school to the Olympic level. Hannula is a former multiple-term president of the American Swimming Coaches Association and a former vice-president of the World Swimming Coaches Association. He is a member of both the American Swim Coaches Association's Hall of Fame and the International Swimming Hall of Fame. Hannula resides in Tacoma, Washington.

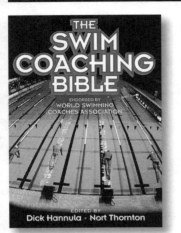
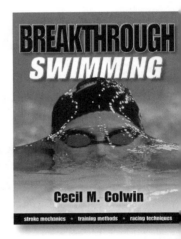
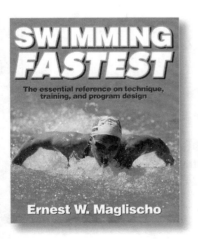